I0061205

Abagusii Wisdom Revisited

Nemwel Mogere Atemba

Nsemia

Copyright @ 2011 Nemwel Mogere Atemba
All Rights Reserved.

No part of this book may be reproduced or utilized in any form or by any means, electronic or mechanical, including photocopying, recording, or by any information storage and retrieval system, without permission in writing from the publisher.

This book is sold subject to the condition that it shall not, by way of trade or otherwise, be re-sold, hired out, or otherwise circulated without the publisher's prior consent in any form of binding or cover other than that in which it is published and without a similar condition including this condition being imposed on the subsequent purchaser.

Editor: Christopher Okemwa
Cover Design: Danielle Pitt
Cover Design Concept: Abel Murumba
Illustrations: Abel Murumba
Design and Layout: Truphena Matunda
Production Consultant: Matunda Nyanchama

Note to Librarians:
A Cataloguing record for this book is available from the Library and Archives Canada.

ISBN: 978-1-926906-03-4 Paperback

First Edition February 2011
Published By **Nsemia Inc. Publishers (www.nsemia.com)**

DEDICATION

To my three children Nyakerario, Nyaata and Nyasani, who were born and brought up in the urban setting, did not have the advantage of hearing and speaking the Abagusii wisdom on a daily basis.

Likewise to all urbanites and Diaspora children who may marvel at the agility of oratory in Ekegusii.

TABLE OF CONTENTS

PREFACE

The renowned African writer Chinua Achebe, once wrote that "among the Ibo, the art of conversation is regarded very highly and that proverbs are the palm oil with which words are eaten". (Things fall apart). I have confirmed this statement to be equally true among the Abagusii.

Proverbs come in handy in all aspects of conversations: instructions, advice, negotiation, persuasion, counseling and defence of oneself against accusations. Where one wields an appropriate proverb, he/she leaves an indelible impression as compared to that one who 'beats about the bush' trying to explain an idea. Proverbs epitomize what experience has taught our elders and ancestors, hence a reality in life.

In this book, I have endeavoured to collect five hundred Kisii sayings in common use and given each an English interpretation and some exposition on applicability. This work is not exhaustive, but it forms a very profitable knowledge and entertainment reservoir.

My main objective is to preserve the positive heritage and wisdom of our ancestors. The greatest worry is that if this art is not mastered now, our children and future generation shall forget about it completely. This is particularly true in respect to the urbanites, who by virtue of location, do not have regular encounters with Ekegusii language.

In addition, my prayers are that scholars may take interest in researching, studying and recording the various progressive aspects of our history, customs and traditions before the sources become extinct. Then, there shall be available a rich heritage to pass on to the future generations.

ABOUT THE AUTHOR

Mr.. Nemwel Mogere Atemba was born in 1956, to young peasant parents at Boking'oina village in the then larger Kitutu Location, Kisii District. He relocated to Nyansiongo settlement scheme in 1965 and after school in 1977, moved to Nairobi for training and employment, where he has resided to date.

He went to school at Tambacha and Nyansiongo primary schools, Nyanturago Secondary school (where in 1975, he set a record of being the very first student in the school to attain Division one (1) in "O" levels). He proceeded to Machakos Boys High School, Eastern province, where he sat for his "A" levels in 1977. Thereafter, he taught for two years at Manga Girls High School before joining the Kenya Railways Corporation for training in Management and Administration fields.

Mr.. Atemba is currently a practicing Human Resource Consultant with C.P.S (K) and Management Diplomas qualifications.

His early experiences with rural elders and colleagues gave him an urge to learn the art of conversation, of which proverbs and other wise sayings form the core determinants in eloquence.

Mr.. Atemba hopes that this book will be of particular interest to students, teachers, researchers, public speakers, preachers, politicians and Kisii people both in Kenya and those in the Diaspora.

ACKNOWLEDGMENTS

I thank the almighty God for being so gracious to all my positive endeavors. Many thanks goes to the people---preachers, politicians, teachers and administrators--who in many occasions have given speeches, infused with proverbs, thus adding to my repertoire of proverbs. .

My gratitude goes to my late maternal grandmother, Trufena Bosibori Marabu, and my paternal grandmother, MariaRosa Bosibori Atemba, both of who gave me the impression that Ekegusii was a worthy language to study and write in.

I owe much thanks to the following elders who guided me in my fierce search for wisdom: Mwalimu John Atai Marabu of Gesurura, Mzee Rev. Andrea Mbego Nyariki of Nyansakia, Rev. Julius Oanda Kiriama of Miriri, Mzee Mishael Atemba Atemba of Nyansiongo, Mzee Johnson Chuma Obare of Manga, Mzee Samuel Kambi Maiteka of Nyansiongo, Mzee Israel Oturi of Kineni, Mzee Samson Momanyi Rasugu of Nyansiongo, Mr.. Peter Osumo Nyambane of Nairobi, Dr. Wilson Moracha Ntabo of USA, Mr.. Victor Monari of Nairobi and Mr.. Samuel Abuta Nyakundi of Nairobi.These are the people who, while in their company, provided me with the motivation that led me towards the compilation and completion of this work.

In a special way I recognize Mr. Christopher Okemwa, who helped with the translation of these proverbs, metaphors and wise sayings, and also offered valuable contributions to the text of this manuscript.

I salute my wife, Dorcas Kemunto (Bakungu 'mbaya..), for being so patient while I read the content of this manuscript to her as she typed.

v

FOREWORD

I have neither met this author nor read of him. That is, till this manuscript landed on my desk. But I feel like I have known him all my life. He reminds me of my uncle who regales me with Ekegusii sayings whenever I meet him and part with a few shillings for a drink with his mates. Or my grandparents' tales by the fire side after the evening meal. Or that village elder who provided so generously of his wisdom so that I would complete my oral literature project back in high school. You will not know all of these people, yet their knowledge of *Ekegusii* is deep and their willingness to share it gratifying.

Yet, this generation of people with this deep knowledge of Ekegusii and a willingness to share is vast disappearing and with it Ekegusii as a coherent and rich language. Did I say disappear? Yes! It is very hard these days to find anyone of my generation or younger (or even older?) who can comfortably converse in *Ekegusii* without throwing in the occasional English word. But worse, one would have to walk many miles before they can find someone who can weave the words and sayings of *Ekegusii* into the rich conversation I experienced as a young boy.

Mr. Atemba's *"Abagusii Wisdom Revisited"* is therefore a timely and welcome endeavour that should awaken us to the urgent need to recover our language before we lose it forever. The book records Ekegusii wise sayings, proverbs and metaphors with their English translations. The book also lists the *Ekegusii* names of common phenomena such as different colours and names of cattle based on their physical characteristics.

Regarding the latter those who grew up in Gusii would recall that cows were fondly referred to by these names and would respond to them when called. The book also reveals the names of the different types of alcohol depending on their stage of fermentation and wives according to their rank in the marriage. Those who refer to a calender written in English would be delighted to know that Abagusii had words for the different months and days of the year. And that a pot is not just a pot: there is *embiiru, ensiongo, ekegancha, ekeguru, enyakaruga, egetega, egetoono,* and *egetabo.* Such is the richness of *Ekegusii!*

The *Abagusii* have a saying that *"Mominchori 'mi tang'ana mosera' ibu".* This saying is a clarion call for us to stop sitting on our laurels and instead start the urgent task of not only recording our language but recovering it as a source of knowledge, wisdom and, yes, entertainment. Indigenous communities such as the Maori in New Zealand are now seriously engaged in efforts at recovering their language which had almost disappeared thanks to years of colonialism. Renowned novelist Ngugi aa Thiongo has fought to restore the place of African languages and especially his language, Gikuyu. Time has come for Abagusii to take up this good fight. Mr. Atemba makes an important contribution in this journey.

Robert Ochoki Nyamori Ph.D CPA

PROVERBS

A

1. Abamura 'mbanga 'bande, tochaya 'bande. *(Abamura nigo babwekaine abande, tochaya abande).*

All men may not be equally strong; but do not underrate any of them; every locality has its best, hence neither overly praise your own nor underrate others.

2. Abana ne'chisese. *(Abana nabo banga chisese):*

Children are puppies: Children, like puppies, are innocent, naïve and ignorant. They will always insist on having their way, even if they are wrong or admonished. Hence, do not be unduly annoyed with their deeds.

3. Abanda 'mbairokaine; Onchong'a agatama ekworo Kimaiga kayebwate *(Abanda imbairokaine, Onchong'a agatama ekworo ekero Kimaiga ayebwate):*

The rich revere/fear one another as in the case of Onchong'a who fled on noticing Kimaiga's cloak.

Story-line: Once there were two rich men who unknowingly met at the home of a beautiful girl, whom they both intended to woo. Mr.. Onchong'a reported earlier. However, when Mr.. Kimaiga also arrived for the same purpose, Mr.. Onchong'a, who was less wealthy, stealthily walked away without ado.

4. Abande namokwana timonga rigoro riang'ung'uire rikorabia obori mogondo *(Abande namonagokwana timonga rigoro rikong'ung'ura erinde obori bwaraba mogondo):*

Talking too is not similar to a thunderstorm which, when it sounds, finger millet *(wimbi)* in the farm ripens. (Better listen to thunderstorm which brings rain that could ripen *wimbi*, with its benefits, than idle talk, which has no benefit.)

1

5. **Abange 'mbaya, mbuna bariete 'kiane 'nkaigwa bororo**
(Abange n'abaya, kobono nigo bariete ekiane ekagera inkaigwa bobe):
Many people/hands are good, however they consumed my food and I felt pain. (Many hands make work lighter, however, they also come with a cost, commensurate compensation for the work they do; the more hands the higher the cost).

6. **Abaisia 'mbaisia, 'mbasambete egesa ki'omogaka** *(Abaisia n'abaisia, imbasambete egesa kia omogaka):*
Lads will always behave like lads as a result of which they once set ablaze an elder's hut. (This is a warning that lads, being immature, react foolishly and can destroy property; they need to be understood and be given guidance.)

7. **Abasacha 'mbaniberani na 'bakungu 'mbaiborerani** *(Abasacha nigo bakoniberana na abakungu baiborerana):*
While Men share wealth with one another, women beget children for one another. This proverb was used to encourage communal sharing, generosity and being one's brother's keeper.
Story-line: Kisii customary law demanded that whenever a young man took a wife but had no cattle for dowry, his relatives could be forced to contribute whatever number of cattle was required for dowry. Similarly, if in a home a co-wife's daughter got married, the dowry would be used to pay her step son's dowry. In both situations, no consent was sought from the affected persons.

8 .**Abaya 'mbainse** *(Abaya imbaria bare inse, baria bakure):*
The good ones belong to "the underneath"/the earth / grave. (This proverb is used when a generous person dies with an intention to console the bereaved.)

9. **Aka 'moko akworokie amarwa ase are** *(Aka omoko egere akworokererie ase amarwa are):*

Beat up a brother-in-law so that he can reveal the whereabouts of liquor.

Storyline: A story is told about a brother-in-law who was beaten up while asking for his sister's remaining dowry. He had to call the elders from both sides to arbitrate the dispute. During the session, much beer was drunk to the delight of all participants. Hence some harm to one person has benefit to the other.

10. **Amarwa 'ntabichu.** *(Amarwa intabichu):*

Liquor unties the tongue. (When the wine "gets in", the "wit gets out". Liquor opens people up to loose talk and even to obscene language.)

11. **Ankio mosuko kande.** *(Ankio naende tonyore akande):*

May tomorrow bring forth another one. (This is used to encourage or bless an effort even though its outcome is uncertain).

12. **Ase ogokwera 'maiga are** *(Ase ogokwera nao ogosanera ogende/nao amaiga are):*

The place where one is going to die at is attractive and alluring. (A place that bears a great risk is the most alluring. This is a warning against short term pleasures which portend danger.)

3

13. **Ase ribego rire nao chinsoti chigosangererekana** *(Ase eng'iti y'orosana ekwerete nao chinsoti chigosangererekana):*

Vultures gather wherever there is a carcass. (People assemble where they derive benefits from e.g. festivals and celebrations).

B

14. **Baba 'mbaba, na tata 'ntata, bonsi n'abaya 'mbito bikobora** *(Abaibori bonsi nigo n'abaya n'ebinto bikobora tokobaa):*

Mother will ever remain mother and father will ever remain father, both are good; it is only that we lack enough wealth to appease them. (Parents are so precious that we are supposed to provide for them. However, we don't have enough wealth to appease them satisfactorily or meet all their needs as we would wish.)

15. **Baba n'omuya ondereire kwaa, na 'magega a'boronge na 'ngobo chi'marera** *(Baba n'omuya ekiagera andereire kwaa amo n'amagega n'echingobo chimarera):*

My mother is good, because she has cared me, carrying me on her back with soft leather clothes. (This is a praise and blessing to one's mother).

16. **Babasi 'mbanga 'bana, ko'bono 'mbanga Bwana** *(Ababasi nigo banga abana, korende bono nigo banga Bwana):*

People from Bobasi clan are like "children", however nowadays they are like lords.

Story-line: This is a satirical proverb that teases the Bobasi clan. The main clans of Omogusii are Bobasi, Bogetutu, Bogirango, Bonchari, Bomachoge, Nyaribari. A story is told of how Mobasi (anncestor of Ababasi) was requested to slaughter a cow for visitors. He skinned the cow with a cut

4

on the back, striping the skin towards the feet, which is not the routine it is done. By doing so, the work was completed fast, but the hide was damaged. The elders quipped: "This is childish work." From this incident, the Ababasi, continued being referred to as "children." However, in the 1960's the Ababasi, who have substantially succeeded in business, especially in Kisii town, became richer than other people. This helped change the impression people had of them. So when they are referred to as "childish," they retort by saying, "despite the past, nowadays we are the lords."

17. **'Bagenki bakwa na 'bitonga bi 'motwe** *(Abagenki nigo bagokwa n'ebitonga kabire emetwe yabo):*
Back-biters die holding firmly to the baskets on their heads.
 (People who back-bite others will stop (with loads on their heads) and keep on talking thereby wearing themselves out. This is a warning to them to mind their own business.)

18. **Bagirango 'mabera, ko! ching'ereru   ne   chia Bogirango rogoro** *(Abagirango mbare n'amabera, kobono ching'ereru nigo chire Bogirango rogoro):*
Bogirango clan has generally kind-hearted people, however, the stubborn ones reside in the North.
Story-line: This is satire. It talks of people from North Bogirango who do not agree easily with any issue even if it is of some benefit to them. Instead of readily agreeing on an issue, they will first consult with their relatives even on trivial matters. So when a person from Bogirango objects to something, you better give up trying to convince him/ her, since no amount of persuasion will achieve that.

19. **'Bakungu 'mbaya n'emenwa yabasaririe** *(Abakungu n'abaya korende n'emenwa ekobasaria):*
Women are of great value; however, their "mouths" are their

5

Achilles heel. (This is in reference to perceptions that women gossip and nag more.)

20. **'Bakungu tibana gotogia onde, otango 'mbatogetie nyamani** *(Abakungu tibana gotogia monto onde bwensi, onye nabo ananga imbatogetie omosacha obarageretie n'amani):*
Women have never praised their men no matter what great things their men do for them; if it were so, they would have praised a man who fed them on liver.
Story-line: Once there was a man who, in his quest to please his wives, kept on improving the quality of meat he brought home. Nevertheless, these women would always have something negative to say about the meat: "too bonny," "too fat," "too lean," "too tough," "too rotten," and so on. Eventually, he decided to buy the liver for them, which was not only rare but also costly. Despite the effort and the cost, they had something to say: "This is too soft and tasteless." He finally gave up.

21. **'Banto 'bamo 'mbachayani** *(Abanto abamo nigo bagochayana):*
People of the same blood despise one another. (Familiarity breeds contempt. A prophet has honour except in his village).

22. **'Banto 'mba 'maiso, 'mioyo etamanyaini** *(Abanto n'abamaiso n'emioyo etamanyaini):*
We judge people by their appearances, little do we know of their hearts. (You can not trust people by their appearance, or what they say; beware of people's flattery, for not all that glitters is gold.)

23. **Banto 'mbaumerani, 'mbitunwa bitakoumerana** *(Abanto nigo bakoumerana, ko bono n'ebitunwa bitari koumerana):*

People do meet; it is only mountains/hills that don't.
(This is a warning to criminals and defaulters: You can't hide for long enough, since you are likely to meet the people you have wronged in the past.)

24. **'Basacha tibana kobisana 'mbara** *(Abasacha tibari kobisana chimbara):*
Men do not conceal their ugly spots (secrets) from one another. (Men disclose their failures and weaknesses openly to one another. They do not get embarrassed when making a request for something from other men, for instance borrowing a small amount of money.)

25. **'Basamaro 'mabega 'mabe, ko 'mabwata 'maya** *(Abasamaro nigo bakobega obokima bobe, ko bono babwata egasi buya):*
Basamaro clansmen apportion themselves a big proportion of ugali, but are hard working.
Story-line: This is a satire. Bosamaro is one of the main clans of Bogirango. These people are "renowned" for their strength. One man can till a whole acre of shamba alone in the morning session and in the afternoon he splits firewood for three homes. However, they are equally renowned for consuming large quantities of food. Once upon a time, there was a father and his son who went to visit their prospective in-laws. The host women served ugali first and went to the kitchen to fetch stew. When they returned they found an empty plate. The two visitors from Bosamaro clan had consumed the "dry ugali" *within seconds! The pride to-be was so up-set that she turned down the marriage. "How can I be able to cook enough food for these people?" she wondered.*

26. **'Baturi 'mbaibi, 'mbauti batakoiba** *(Abaturi n'abaibi korende abauti barabwo tibari koiba):*

Blacksmiths are all thieves; it is the fire fanners who do not steal. (A blacksmith will readily sell items in his possession items to any prospective customer, despite the items being paid for in advance. However, the fire fanner (his assistant) may not be aware of this. This proverb is used to warn people from generalizing the characteristics of a trade. This is to say not all those involved in blacksmith skills are dishonest.)

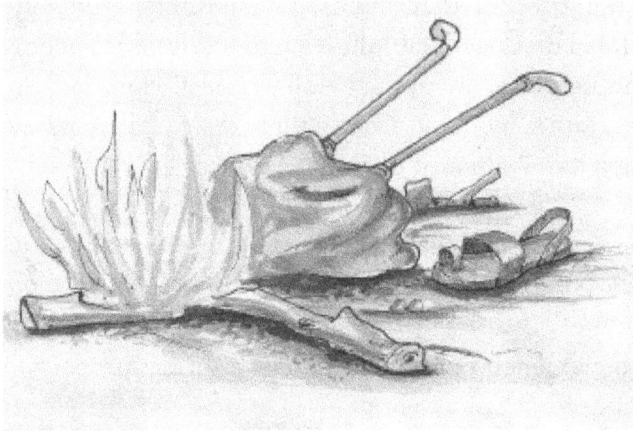

27. **Beka 'boko bwa'mbura toigame** *(Beka oboko erinde embura egotwa twaigama):*
Develop some in-law relationship, whose home may offer us shelter during the rainy season. (In their sojourns, people used to shelter from the rain in homes of relatives, including in-laws. Relations come with benefits, however small.)

28. **Binto 'mbia mochi'kare** *(Ebinto n'ebi omonto ogochia kare):*
Wealth belongs to the one who lives for long. (This is a warning to the miser: use your wealth and live well, for one is not permanent in this world.)

29. **Binto 'mbiang'ora, 'nsagasaga bikwanga** *(Ebinto n'ebiang'ora; n'esagasaga bikwanga):*
Success prefers orderliness and patience, but it shuns haste

and chaos. (Hurry! Hurry! has no blessings. Wealth or success demands for patience; it abhors haste, recklessness and chaos.)

30. **'Binto 'mbikone; 'sasati ekaibora 'mache, na morero okaibora 'ibu** *(Ebinto n'ebikone, buna esasati eiborete amache, na omorero oiborete ribu):*
Wonders never cease; the elephant grass "produces" water while fire produces ashes. (This refers to experiences in life that is full of paradoxes.)

31. **Binto 'mbiontigera, n'ontigeire agatigera onde** *(Ebinto n'ebi' ontigera, na ontigera ocha otigera onde):*
Wealth is inherited and the heir would leave it for someone else. (Wealth changes hands; do not waste it; save it for others. The proverb encourages sharing; discourages greed.)
32. Binto 'nganda, mogeni agocha ariera nyeni, mosuko mori yagonkire (Ebinto n'echinganda, omogeni agocha oriera ching'eni ekero emori ekagonkete):
Wealth fades; on some occasions when a calf has suckled all the milk a visitor may be served with only vegetables. (No one stays rich all the time.)

33. **Birenge 'nyanche** *(Ebirenge biane inyanche):*
 My legs may you support me. (Someone utters this when he/she is fleeing from danger.)

34. **'Bokabara 'mbomuma bokagera 'ngatandora engobo yane** *(Obokabara nigo bore buna emuma, imbwagerete ingatandora engobo yane):*
Naughtiness is like a curse, it made me tear my beautiful dress for no good reason. (This refers to regrets one utters later after reflecting on the past.)
Story-line: A story is told of a girl who refused to be married to a particular man because she considered him poor. She

tore her dress to express her outrage. However her brothers forced her to live with him. Later, this man was crowned chief of the village. Now, during the home coming ceremony, the wife was heard admonishing herself for the unbecoming behaviour she had exhibited when she married him.

35. **'Bokumu 'ndwari** *(Obokumu n'endwari):*
Shyness is a disease. (An expression aimed at encouraging open communication. When one has a problem, he/she should share it out with others, lest it torments him/her just like a disease.)

36. **Bogetutu n'enda y'enchogu** *(Bogetutu nigo enga enda y'enchogu):*
Bogetutu clan is like the "stomach of an elephant".
Story-line: Bogetutu clan is regarded as the cradle of Gusii community where members of all other clans can be found. Since all other clans live there it is referred to as an "elephant's stomach", where all kinds of plants and grass are digested. Why are members of other clans living in Bogetutu? It is said that Mogetutu (ancestor of Abagetutu), rather than use his hands to work, liked others to do it for him. These were usually poor people from other clans that did the hewing of wood, fetching of water and the like. Eventually, they ended up staying and hence the reason for representation of all Mogusii clans in Bogetutu. Also during the Kisii movements, people from Bogetutu did not move; they remained at their first settlement. Now when other clans met enemies and retreated they stayed together once again, making Bogetutu the home for members of all clans. Later when they left, some were left behind and lived there to date.

37. **'Bogiri bwa' 'meseke 'mosomba oroche okoria** *(Okogira koria emeseke nase engencho omosomba arorekanete okoyeria):*

For someone to reject beer dregs, he must have seen a slave eating them. (Rich people will tend to reject common foods consumed by poor people, however delicious they may be. For instance a wealthy person may not join the common folks in eating ripe bananas in public. He will give excuses to "protect his dignity".)

38. **'Bogotu tibori gokura** *(Obogotu tibori gokura):*
Old age does not come screaming. (Old age comes without warning. It doesn't announce its coming.)

39. **Bonchari 'nkorera bare tangori e'Manga ebe yaito, erio torande bokemurwa** *(Abanchari inkorera bare ng'a otangori e'Manga ebe eyaito, erio torande buna emurwa):*
The people of Bonchari clan wish that Manga ridge could be part of their land. If it were, then they would occupy it and spread on it like exuberant grass.
Story-line: Manga plateau is a very beautiful landscape in Gusii-land. It is covered by "ekenyoru", ever green soft shining exuberant grass, which is used for thatching wealthy people's houses. It towers above a plain called 'chache', which extends as far as the eye can see, ending at the great Lake Victoria. This was the cradle of Abagusii before their dispersion to their present locations. Now, Bonchari clan occupies lowland lacking specific natural landmarks for identification purposes hence their wish to have a share of Manga plateau.

40. **Bonchari 'nguba chiabokendu, 'monto okoria 'ngubo tacha minto anyue 'mache, n'egesaku akunama** *(Abanchari na abechinguba chia obokendu, omonto okoria engubo tacha minto anywe amache, n'egesaku akunama):*
Bonchari clansmen have a link with cold water, which is why a man who eats a Hippopotamus should not be welcome

11

to share a drink of water in our home; should such a person be welcome, a curse would befall the whole clan.

Story-line: During migrations, a Hippo saved men from Bonchari who were being pursued by Luo enemies. In the chase, the enemies bumped into a hippo, and thought it was the one that they had been chasing and not the men from Bonchari. So they retreated, leaving the exhausted clansmen just hidden at the riverbank, unable to cross the waters. The elders in Bonchari clan thereafter declared the hippo as a sacred animal; it saved their clansmen from their enemies.

41. **'Bonda irareri** *(Obonda nigo bogokorarisereria):*
Wealth is slumber. (Wealth makes one go into sleep. He/she is not awake, or conscious, of other people's plight.)

42. **'Bonda 'mbwo' otarochi** *(Obonda nobworia otarochi):*
Wealth belongs to those who do not see it. (Wealth is best enjoyed by those who do not attach so much importance to it. This is a warning to those who think wealth is everything one needs in life.)

43. **'Bong'aini Mokoronto aroche maisaransa, mosae takoborora n'atenena** *(Obong'aini boria Mokoronto aroche gaikaransete, omosae takoborora n'atenena):*
What an old man sees while seated, a young man can't see it even when standing up. (This refers to the wisdom of the old, given they have more experience than youth.)

44. **'Borabu 'nswenta** *(Oborabu nsweta):*
The world is a massive void. (The world is a big void, such that if one is likely to wander everywhere, and lose oneself in the void, therefore rendering it hard to trace one or making it hard for one to come home in the time one intends. This proverb is uttered when someone is late coming home, or

when someone is late leaving for one's home.)

45. **'Bororo 'mbori bwairongo, ka'botonya riko** *(Obororo n'obori bore irongo, bogotonya gochia eriko):*
Sorrow is like *wimbi* in the loft, which eventually falls into the fire. (*Wimbi* stored up in the loft of the hut suffers the discomfort of smoke and heat, but when it falls into the fire below, it perishes.)

46. **'Bororo 'mbwanyene, eamate echana bosa igo** *(Obororo n'obwa omonyene, k'eamate echana bosa igo):*
Bitterness/sorrow belongs to the bereaved, however the neighbours will only come around to condole with them. (It is the bereaved who feel the pain. Those not affected will only join the bereaved and be with them.)

47. **'Bororo 'nkamati a' maseko** *(Obororo n'ekamati ya amaseko).*
Sorrow is a sister-in-law to Laughter. (This is used as an encouragement in sad moments.)

48. **'Bororo 'mbori goita, 'nkenoro bogokora** *(Obororo tibori goita, n'ekenoro bogokora):*
Sorrow does not kill; it actually fattens. (This is an irony used in encouraging people during sorrowful moments.)

49. **Boterere 'mbori 'momura** *(Oboterere tibori omomura):*
A slippery ground does not respect any man. Even the strongest can fall on a slippery ground. (This is a warning to those who think that their physical strength is everything).

50. **'Bototo bwa'monto** *(Obototo bw'omonto):* One's efforts. (This is an encouragement for one's effort and achievement, no matter how small.)

51. **'Buya bwa ng'ondi 'nsigiti etaratwata** *(Obuya bw'eng'ondi mboria bw'esigiti etaratwata):*
The beauty of a sheep is the ewe that has not given birth. (A woman's beauty is impacted by childbearing.)

52. **Bwabeire 'maiso a'bakungu** *(Bwabeire amaiso y'abakungu):*
It has become "women's eyes". (This refers to dusk when one cannot identify objects clearly. Women who keep late hours panic and keep running on their way home).

53. **Bwaisa koira ebitutu biekone** *(Bwabeire ang'e koira ekero ebitutu bigwekona):*
Behold, its dusk when bushes become mysterious. (This refers to dusk when familiar objects assume menacing shapes).

54. **'Bwanchi 'mbwa' mweri k'omosunte bwabora** *(Obwanchi nobw'ekero ki' omweri, kobono ekero ki'omosunte bobora):*
Love thrives when it shines, e.g. in moonshine; but not in darkness. (When one is rich people would want to associate with one; when one becomes poor, one's popularity wanes, and no one takes interest in the person).

55. **'Bwanchi 'mbwariete Ogeko** *(Obwanchi nigo bwariete Ogeko):*
Love caused Ogeko's death. (What one loves most is what leads one to one's destruction. Love is blind.)

56. **'Bwanchi 'mbwaitete Ogeko, mogoroba o'bikuuro ogochiera nyeni na nko** *(Obwanchi nigo bwaitete Ogeko, mogoroba koyaikire ekero ching'eni n'echinko chigosabanwa):*
Excess kindness/love caused Ogeko's death at dusk when

14

vegetables and firewood are sought for. (Let us not expose ourselves too much even to our intimate friends.)

Story-line: Once there was a very intimate friend of Ogeko who came to visit him and stayed up to late in the evening. At the end of his visit, he bid the host good bye and left, only to come back through the back side of the homestead and entered his cow-shed, intending to steal the host's cow. Noticed, the visitor turned on Ogeko and killed him. Had Ogeko, the host, not extended the friend's stay up to dusk because of his love and kindness, that friend could not have had a chance of familiarizing himself with the homestead and strategize on how to steal from his host, and end up in killing Ogeko, the host.

C

57. Chaga bwangwe 'tureti ko'bwanchwe nyomba *(Chaga bwangwe ase eturei korende bwanchwe mwao):*
Better be despised by your contemporaries but be respected in your family. (Even if your friends despise you, they will change their attitude once they discover that your family respects or disrespects you.)

58. Chaga 'nda ekoreterere *(Chaga enda yao ekoreterere):*
May your own womb bring you trouble.
Let your own "stomach" bring you woes. (Refers to children whose criminal activities bring agony to their parents.)

59. Chaga oene oborwe ogokoenora *(Chaga oene na oborwe oyomino ogokoenora):*
May you be in trouble, but have no kin to come to your help. (This is a curse to a person who does not regard others. If he falls into difficulties he will not have someone to assist.)

60. Chaga orare echia 'motegandi *(Chaga orare echi omotegandi ararete):*
May you sleep like the woodcutter. (A deep sleep that comes because of exhaustion from heavy work.)

61. Chaga osire buna Ombati asirete, agacha akairana n'omorero *(Chaga osiere buna Ombati asirete, magega yaye agacha akairana n'omorero):*
May you disappear like Ombati did and later resurfaced, but "carrying fire".

Story-line: Ombati is the only known person from Gusiiland who was ever taken as a slave by the Arab traders; but was later rescued by the British soldiers enroute to the coast. When he returned home, he was accompanied by British colonialists carrying guns to Gusii land.

62. **Chaga osire buna 'mbori a 'marwa** *(Chaga osire buna embori y'omonto onywete amarwa)*:
May you disappear like the drunkard's goat. (A drunkard goes away to drink, leaving his goat tethered to a tree by the roadside. While away, the goat strains on the rope and manages to tear it, giving it a free reign. When the drunkard comes back, he finds the goat missing.)

63. **Chaga 'semi chia 'gekuro chiateke, chitigare chimoya** *(Chaga chisemi chiegekuro chiateke, chitigare chimoya)*:
May your calabashes break to expose your privacy. (Do not be proud; pride comes before a fall.)

64. **Chiaita 'mogeni, chiaita n'onka** *(Nigo chigoita omogeni, na boigo chiaita na oyonka)*:
They beat the visitor; they also beat the host. (A problem should be shared equally between the visitors and the hosts. Necessity knows no boundaries.)

65. **Chiakumeire Moraa o'Kiage, akama 'ng'ombe akama 'mbori** *(Chiakumeire Moraa, 'mosubati O'Kiage, okoba agokama chiombe naende okama chimbori)*:
Fame has come to Moraa, daughter of Kiage, who milks both cows and goats. (This is uttered by co-wives. Here Moraa, daughter of Kiage, is blessed with both children and livestock, hence the sinister reference by her co-wives.)

66. **Chiera 'mang'ana rooti** *(Gwachiera amang'ana ng'ora):*
Go slow on issues. (Think, investigate, research before you act. Do not act on rumours or hearsay.)

67. **Chiesa Bonyankanga, ko tochiesa Bonubi gati** *(Mochera abanyankanga, ko tomochera abanubi):*
It is safer to cause trouble in the police precincts, than causing trouble at the village of Nubia. The proverb is used to advise one to pick his/her fights carefully and avoid those where defeat is certain.
Story-line: In the olden days in Kisii town, there were two spectacular residential estates adjacent to one another: Administration Police and the village of Nubia. Thieves used to raid the homes in the two estates from time to time. The thieves arrested around the police precinct were punished (e.g. canned) and released, but woe unto those caught stealing within and around the village of Nubia: Their hands and legs were bound and beaten to death.

68. **Chiombe n'amakabe** *(Chiombe nachio chigoonchora oboiri):*
"Cattle" are responsible for intertwined relations.
Story-line: The Gusii people are very cautious about marriages stemming from same blood relations. No marriage is allowed to even a remotely distant relation. It is considered both incestuous and sacrilegious. However, there are some incidents where relations stemming out of the in-laws are ignored and such is blamed on dowry (cattle). For example, if a father's third wife comes from Botabori clan, any of his sons may marry from the same clan, except the sons of that third wife.

69. **Chiombe 'mbe na 'mbe, chiabutoire Nyankuru 'kiara**

(Chiombe nabo chire chimbe, chiagerire Nyankuru obutoirwe ekiara):

Cattle are bad, so bad that they have caused the loss of Nyankuru's finger. (This refers to the envy between brothers over the ownership of cattle.)

Story-line: A story is told of two brothers who could not agree on the sharing of their sisters' dowry. They quarreled and fought one another, resulting into one of them having his finger chopped off.

E

70. Eamate n'engiya ekogera 'mwana achega *(Eamate n'engiya ekiagera ekogera omwana ochega):*
Neighbours are good, they tolerate a child's troublesomeness. (Neighbours take care of, and tolerate children, even if the children are stubborn.)

71. Ebioto nabitwora boire, 'ng'ombe nabo ekonywa 'mache *(Ebioto nabitwora boire, eng'ombe nabo ekonywa amache):*
The croaking of frogs do not prevent csow from drinking water. (Threats of the weak do not deter the strong.)

72. Ebirama 'mbibisete 'mange *(Ebirama nigo bibisete amang'ana amange):*
There is a lot we don't know in every hut/house. (There are many hidden problems in all families.)

73. Ebichuria 'mbire na 'mang'ana *(Ebichuria nigo bire na amang'ana amange):*
Huts conceal many problems. (Every family has problems or issues that are not known by others outside it.)

74. Echiro ya'torekire!:
The market has exploded! (This refers to a commotion masterminded or created by thieves on a market day, thereby causing confusion, so that it becomes easy for them to steal.)

75. Eeri nyamagwari yang'o? Torochi eng'ina nyabisembe? *(Eeri eye ere na amagwari n'eyang'o? Rora eng'ina ere n'ebisembe):*

To whom does this spotted bull belong? Don't you see its checkered mother? (Children take after their parents).

76. **Eeri tiyana kwana marara** *(Eeri teri kwana ka eraire):*
A bull does not bellow while lying down. (Men are supposed to be strong, enduring, and believed to defy sickness or exhaustion. Therefore even a sick man cannot wait for people to come to see him in his bed, or bed-room; instead he will struggle to lift himself from his bed, or drag himself out of his bedroom, to meet his sympathizers.)

77. **Eganyete tiyana kwoma** *(Ey'eganyete teri kwoma):*
It doesn't dry up when it is still waiting. (One should never give-up while waiting to be served. Patience does not wear someone off.)

78. **Egechure 'nkiarabete etebe y'Omboga** *(Egechure nigo kiarabete etebe ya Omboga):*
An antelope got used to Omboga's tin (Scarecrow).
Story-line: Mr.. Omboga was a farmer who had discovered that an antelope could be frightened by both the sight and sound of a tin. He hung one to scare antelopes at his farm. The trick worked for a while, but as time passed the antelope got used to it and started destroying his crops again. Familiarity breeds contempt.

79. **Egekondo 'nki'eng'enterete 'mbura ng'eti** *(Egekondo nigo kieng'entete okoba embura yaingete ko bono egaeta):*
A monkey committed suicide because of rain that never fell.
Story-line: One day a monkey was terribly rained on. The following day when dark clouds formed, he feared that it would rain on him again as it did the previous day. He decided to hang himself. However, the wind changed direction and swept away the clouds. It did not rain.

80. **Egesoera nyomba** *(Egento omonto agosoera nyomba):*
Something to have when coming home. (This is a term given to a small token (gift), usually food carried by a man in order to invoke a welcome from a wife/mistress. It may be bananas, mangoes, biscuits, sugar or meat.)

81. **Egesomo ngokinia kere, ngetakong'ainiyia** *(Egesomo nigo kegokinia buya, korende tikeri kong'ainiyia):*
Isolated homes provide atmosphere for children's growth, but not conducive for the acquisition of wisdom. (Remote/isolated homes/areas do not provide necessary exposure for intellectual stimulation. The lesson here is that people learn from other people.)

82. **Egetinkinye ekeng'aini kerigie oboundi keagache, 'mbura egotwa gesoe mwaye** *(Egetinkinye okoba kere ekeng'aini nigo gekorigia oboundi kiagacha, erinde embura kegotwa giasoa mwaye):*
The wise wren gathers grass to thatch "its house" in advance, so that it shelters in it when it rains. (This is pride expressed by someone who is successful. It is a lesson for one to be prepared for adversity.)

83. **Egia'koboko 'nkia'monwa are** *(Ekere ase okoboko nigo kere are korwa ase omonwa):*
What is at hand is actually far from the mouth. (Never be contented with what you have not secured or fully accomplished.)

84. **Egiasireire 'nchera rogoro, kerigerie 'nchera maate** *(Egento giasireire enchera ere rogoro, rirorio kerigerie ase enchera ya maate):*
When you cannot find something on one side of the road, try

the opposite side. (Do not be confined to only one course of action; always find an alternative). *(Also: ekiaborire 'nchera rogoro, kerigerie 'nchera maate (egento keria kiaborire ensemo ya enchera rogoro, kerigerie ensemo ya enchera maate):* that which you cannot locate on one side of the path could be found on the other side.)

85. **Egiasinyire 'botongore (tureti) getunyere Nyamberi na Keore o'mwabo** *(Ekina keria giasinyire abatongore (abatureti) rirorio getunyere Nyamberi na Keore omwabo):*
If a case defeats the village elders, refer it to Justice Numbery and his brother Justice Calley. The wisdom here is that one should not give up before pursuing all avenues.
Story-line: Justice Numbery and Justice Calley were colonial court judges known for their quick action on cases.

86. **Egienchara n'engi ekogeitera** *(Egento kegotoka ekero gienchara engi nero ekogera giaiterwa):*
What we get during famine ends up being spilt by a housefly. (A scarce commodity, e.g. milk, mostly in a poor man's home, is prone to accident. It ends up consumed by the flies.)

87. **Eguto yaremera enyang'au** *(Eguto nigo ekoremera enyang'au):*
An ant-bear digs a den for the hyena. (Reference injustice and unfairness. The proverb condemns oppression meted upon weak members of society by the rich and strong.)

88. **Ekeenene 'nkia mokungu 'morogi ona 'bamura** *(Ekeenene ne kia omokungu ore omorogi na boigo obwate abamura):*
Arrogance belongs to a witch with many sons. (A reference to arrogant people who bank their security on the number and strength of their relatives.)

89. **Ekeumbu kiaare 'nkegundi boba** *(Ekeumbu kere aare nigo gekogundia oboba):*
A far away fertile place usually has its mushrooms rotten before they can be harvested. (People do not benefit from good things that are far from their reach.)

90. **Eke ne 'kemama!** *(Eke ne ekemama):*
This is a hard rock! (This is a complex/complicated matter/problem.)

91. **Ekiao 'nkunyunyu, ekiabande 'nsongora igoti** *(Ekiao nigo ogokeria kore nkunyunyu korende ekiabande gwasongora rigoti):*
Yours is eaten in quietness, while someone else's you stretch your neck. (Mean/selfish people are not open to sharing what they have, but desire to share with others what they do not possess.)

93. **Eki'ogosimeka nakio okogesa** *(Egento ogosimeka naende nakio okogesa):*
What you plant is what you harvest. The benefit you get is equal to the effort you have put into something.)

94. **Eki'omogoko n'omwana ogatoire** *(Egento omogoko abwate n'omwana oye okogera otoa):*
What belongs to a miser/selfish person is shared out because of his/her child. (This is commonly used during celebrations for children e.g. birthdays, initiations, and weddings, where a mean parent must invite neighbours and friends to share in his/her food.)

95. **Eki'omoisia n'omotwe igoro gekogundera korwa** *(Egento omoisia abwate nigo gekogunda korwa omotwe):*
What belongs to a lad rots from the head. (Boys are careless and damage anything given to them.)

96. **Ekogota n'okoria 'nda** *(Omonto ogotire nigo akoria chinda):* The aged bite lice. (The elderly people, due to old age, cannot keep themselves tidy, and therefore wear dirty clothes at times invested with lice. They have to bite them.)

97. **Embunde yaitete Onchong'a na Matara o'mwabo n'amagachi egachire** *(Embunde eyere yaitete Onchong'a amo na Matara omwabo nigo egachire amagachi):* The bullet that killed both Onchong'a and his brother Matara is still kept in up in the ceiling. (This refers to a revenge act still waiting to be carried out between enemy clans.)

98. **Enda n'embe yarusetie ekeongo igoro, kegaika inse** *(Enda n'embe nigo yarusetie ekeongo igoro, egakereta inse):* A stomach is bad; it made an eagle descend from the sky to the ground. (This refers to the extent one goes to get food.)

99. **Enda nero amaebi** *(Enda nigo ere amaebi):* The stomach (food) is the love potion. (The wife who cooks good food is always loved by her husband.)

100. **Enda n'esese** *(Enda nigo enga esese):* A stomach is a dog. (This refers to hunger which, when temporarily satisfied, one forgets it will ever happen again.)

101. **Enda n'etagachi** *(Enda nigo ere etagachi):* A stomach is a stadium. (Refers to all kinds of foods and drinks that are simultaneously consumed by one person. It is especially used when one over eats and throws up.)

102. **Endeu yaria enoru (Egento ekereu nigo** *gekoria ekenoru):* The thin (lean) one eats the fat one. (A weak person might defeat a strong one in a contest, as in the Biblical story of David & Goliath.)

103.   **Eng'areka 'yagerete bokayia** *(Eng'areka nero yagerete obokima bokayia):*
Envious competition brought about cooked ugali.
Story-line: In a polygamous home, it was usually the practice that, when one wife was on maternity, the other nursed and cooked for her. Now, a story is told of how one envious woman decided to maliciously over-cook a meal and serve it hot to harm her co-wife. Instead, the co-wife put up more weight and desired more. Eventually, she discovered that her malice was the cause of the co-wife's good health. She confessed of it and henceforth everybody adopted the new cooking style. That is how people started cooking ugali.

104. **Eng'era ntindi ne'goonchwa ng'aya** *(Eng'era entindi nero egoonchwa ching'aya):*
A fierce buffalo is usually speared by many hunters to provide shields.   (Normally, the stubborn ones are the ones who are targeted.)

105. **Eng'ombe n'esereti** *(Eng'ombe enoru nokoba ekoria esereti engiya):*
A cow is "grass". (For a cow to grow healthy, it must get enough and plenty of grass. A person who acquires a good job, or a good business, also acquires health).

106. **Engoro 'nderere, nainche nkorerere** *(Engoro inderere omwana oyo, erinde nainche inkorerere):*
God, may you watch over my child, and I will also nurse it for you. (This is a mother's prayer for a newly-born child). (Also: *Rioba 'nderera.*)

107. **Eng'uko enyeanyi eborwa 'maswa** *(Eng'uko ebwate obweanchi nigo ekoborwa amaswa):*

A proud mole has no beddings. (This refers to a proud woman who does not keep her house in order.)

108. **Enibo na' maboko ere** *(Enibo nase amaboko ere):*
Wealth is in the hands. (Nothing can deter a physically healthy person from acquiring wealth. This is an encouragement to those who are lazy.)

109. **Ensanako 'yaitete omoriakari** *(Ensanako nigo yaitete omoriakari):*
The safari ant did kill a bride.
Story-line: *(A story is told of a bride who was being bitten by an ant. To keep her dignity she endured the pain, until she collaped. This warns us not to die because of safeguarding our dignity. Be yourself always.)*

110. **Nse y'abande 'nkenama gesabire, menya bosonsogoro** *(Ense y'abande n'ekenama gesabire, yemenye kore bisonsogoro):*
Living in foreign land is synonymous to a borrowed thigh, live on it ready to flee. (When in a foreign land be prepared to flee (using your legs/thigh). This is an advice for foreigners to behave humbly/friendly when in a foreign land and be aware that the hospitality can end any time.)
(Also: *'Nse y'abande 'nkenama gesaririe!*)

111. **Ensinyo mana kwana (kwoga), 'mbamura etabwati** *(Ensinyo gekona gokwanwa, na abamura etabwati):*
A neighbourhood, whose people are always wailing, has no warriors. (Enemies take advantage of weakness. Warriors could exterminate enemy raids.)

112. **Enyang'au enyoba 'nkwe'gotera ere** *(Enyang'au ere enyoba nigo ekomenya amatuko amange goika yagota):*

A cowardly hyena lives up to old age. (Be humble to avoid victimization.) (cf: cowards live long!)

113. **Enyimbo ya'momura 'moke 'momura 'monene okoyetarera** *(Enyimbo y'omomura omoke n'omomura omonene okoyetarera):*
A younger brother's rod is often used by a senior brother. (This refers to the respect that is expected between age groups.)

114. **Enyomba n'eyemo n'etoto yaye'bagire** *(Enyomba nigo ere eyemo, korende n'etoto ekoyebaga):*
The house is one unit, but it is the partitioning that has divided it.   (Reference to one tribe which has several clans or a home with many wives.)

115. **Enyongo 'ngesieri egwatekera** *(Enyongo yarure are nabo egwatekera gesieri):*
A pot breaks at the doorstep/threshold. (Don't count yourself successful just because you have almost made it. Do not count your chicks before they hatch.)

116. **Enuko enkuru nero egoita** *(Enuko egokurerana nero ekobua):*
A group that warns (alerts) one another in advance usually wins/kills. (This refers to unity and co-ordination among the people of the same clan. Unity and coordination can enable them win their enemies if they invade the.)

117. **Esemi imagega ere** *(Chisemi nigo chigocha magega ekero omonto akorire egento ki'oboriri):*
Wisdom comes after. (Wisdom comes after one has made a mistake. This refers to the power of hindsight.)

118. **Esemo 'yariete eyende** *(Esemo nigo yariete eyende):*
A brother-in-law "ate"/betrayed his other brother-in-law.
(Refers to taking advantage of relations.)

119. **'Sese eaberi 'yairete 'twoni Bogere/Esese enkungu nero yairete ensacha Bogere** *(Esese eaberi iyarusetie etwoni korwa bogore):*
A female dog lured a male dog into Luo land. (This refers to love and infatuation. A woman is a powerful bait, as in the Biblical story of Samson and Delilah.)
(Also: *Esese eaberi 'yarusetie 'twoni Bogere!*)

120. **'Sese 'mbe (entindi) neyangori 'ntambe** *(Esese eyere embe nigo egosiberwa engori entambe):*
A fierce dog is tethered with a long rope. (This refers to an obstinate person, who loses all his friends.)

121. **Sese 'mbe teri bogeni** *(Esese embe teri gwesika ekero ere ase obogeni):*
A bad dog respects no host. (This refers to bad manners displayed by uncultured visitors.)

122. **Esese 'maria bonyira, tari 'mosemia eborire, nabo eture igo** *(Esese ekoria obonyira, tari omosemia eborire, nabo etongire igo):*
The reason why a dog eats faeces is not that it has no advisor; it is its nature. (Some habits cannot be changed, just tolerate them.)

123. **Etachi korina tiga erie chintobera inse** *(Eye etari konyara korina yetige erie chiria chiatobeire inse):*
Since it won't climb, allow it to eat the ripened fruits on the ground. (A lazy person need not complain when neglected. He should be contented with what is available, e.g., stale fruit on the ground.)

124. **Etari na 'kemincha etirerie 'keene** *(Eng'ombe etari na ekemincha yetige etirerie ekeene):* Let the tailless cow dance with its stump. (Disability is not inability. Even disabled persons need to enjoy themselves.)

125. **Etagweti eng'ina n'ekogwa ise** *(Egento getari kogwa ng'ina nigo gekogwa ise):*
If it does not take after its mother, it takes after its father. (Like father like son. Children take after the parents.)
(Also: *Nyang'era 'ndotungi, na mori yaye 'ndotungi.*)

126. **Eyabande 'magoroba egoosia** *(Eng'ombe yabande imaragoba egoosia):*
The production of milk from another person's cow ceases in the evening. (What does not belong to you can be taken away any time by the owner without notice; do not rely on it. Never be contented with what is offered free by someone.)

127. **Ey'ekoroma 'ngete egoserererwa** *(Egento gekoroma n'egete kegosererwa):*
That which bites is repulsed using a stick. (When dining with the devil use a long spoon. The wisdom is stay away from evil people.)

128. **Ey'ekwana 'mbwango ekoegwa emori** *(Eng'ombe ekwana imbwango ekoegwa emori):*
An animal that cries earlier is the one that is given a calf. (The squeaking wheel is the one that gets oiled.)

129. **Ey'etang'aine ebuneke, ey'ekorwa nyuma eyeete**
(Eyere etang'aine ebuneke okogoro, eyere ekorwa magega eete):
Let the one ahead injure/break its leg and the one following behind go ahead of it. (This is a warning to competitors not to be over-confident when leading and also an advice to those behind not to give up.)

130. **Ey'etang'aine n'etang'aine** *(Eyere etang'aine nigo etang'aine):*
The one which is ahead will finish the race ahead of others. (This is an encouragement to the leader to keep a head.)

G

131. **Gambera omuya togambera omobe, gokogambera omobe nguru kwemarire** *(Gambera omonto oyore omuya, togambera oyore omobe, gokogambera omobe ne chinguru kwemarire):*
It is recommended that you advise a wise person and not a foolish one; if you a fool you will be wasting your energy/time.(Some people are meant for punishment and not advice.)

132. **Ge' kwaborwa, o'Mogwasi ing'aakoire** *(Gakwaborirwe omosacha ogokonywoma tiga omogwasi akonywome):*
If you cannot be married at home, you will be married by a Gwasiman (far away!).
Story-line: In the olden days, Suba men preferred to marry spinsters from Gusii land. Therefore, girls who delayed to get married because no one had proposed around home, ended up in Subaland where life was even more comfortable. It is an advice to girls never to worry when they are over-age and are not married.

133. Genda na 'bwari 'buya, na onywe 'mache 'maya *(Genda n'obwari obuya, na onywe amache amaya):*
Go in peace, and may you always drink pure water. (This is a blessing pronounced by a father to a newly married daughter just before departure to start a new life with her husband.)

134. Gesere giachencha Iberia *(Gesere nigo kegochencha Iberia):*
Gesere laughs at Iberia. (These were two opposite hills, which were inferred to be laughing at each other when both were set on fire. This is advice not to despise others since we all have our weaknesses.)

135. Gesimba tikiana koriera ase kemenyete *(Egesimba tikeri koriera ase kemenyete):*
A jackal never eats/kills where it lives. (If a jackal steals from nearby, it is likely to be hunted down and killed. One should keep his reputation in the area in which he lives.)

136. Gesinsi 'ntwoni ng'era *(Egesinsi n'etwoni eng'era):*
 An insect is a great buffalo. Do not despise unimportant/small/young people. A small man can win in a fight. Similarly, an "unimportant" person can turn out to be useful in some situations. David killed Goliath in a fight.

137. Gesio 'nkia 'moba na 'masinga *(Egesio ne kia amoba na amasinga):*
Blessings for both bigger and smaller mushrooms. (This refers to a blessing pronounced by an elder to a young person because of the assistance he has provided him.)

138. Getari 'nkiamwabo kende *(Egetari n'ekiamwabo ekende):* One piece is a kin to another. (People are similar. We are one people, so let us love and be kind to one another).

139. Getiiro 'nke mogondo, ko 'moserengeti ore eero
(Egetiro ne kia'mogondo, korende omoserengeti n'oyore eero):
He that encounters a "hill" (challenge) in the farm, leads chatting in the dinning room. (This refers to a lazy person who consumes more food than others.)

140. Getureri gia 'nchara 'ndwari *(Ekegotura enchara n'endwari):*
That which follows starvation is a disease. (Famine triggers diseases. This refers to negligence of elderly people and children. Without food it is easy for them to lack immunity and become sick.)

141 Getutu 'nkere 'maiso *(Egetutu nkere na amaiso):*
A bush has eyes. (This refers to things done in secrecy, which later are unearthed/revealed/discovered.)

142. Geutere giote, gekobamboka, gekobambokere
(Egiatwererwe geutere giote, erinde gekobamboka gekobambokere):
Build fire, allow it (antelope) to warm, when it stirs, it will turn against you: (This refers to a person who has no thanks and assaults the benefactor. It reflects the fact that the very people whom you have helped are the ones who work for your downfall.)

143. Gochia 'maguta motwe (gochia iburu) *(Ogochia amaguta motwe):*
To be anointed with oil on the head. (This is a rite of passage from childhood to adulthood through initiation.)

144. Gochiatacha 'nchianywa *(Ekero chiatachire nabo enga buna nigo chianywa):*
Since they (cows) have stepped in the water, then it is as

good as they have drank the water (All people, both with one or many sins, are all referred to as sinners. There is no sin that is smaller than the other. If you commit one small sin you are still referred to as a sinner.)

145. **Gokenakena, 'nkwa 'mbeba ere na itete** *(Ogokenakena nigo kore okwembeba ere na itete):*
Panicking and nervousness is for the rat that is conveying a millet husk. (A reference to unsettled mind/confusion out of curiosity of an impending danger.)

146. **Gokobeka Mokeira ibega 'kebeera kwereteire** *(Gokobeka Mokeira ibega riao ne'kebera kwaretire ase ore):*
If you place Mokeira close to you, then you have brought a boil on your body.
Story-line: "Mokeira" is a person from Bokeira sub-clan of Bogirango. This refers to assisting or guiding someone, with an aim of making him independent. However, he later stubbornly demands a share of your property, as in the story of the "Arab and the camel".

147. **Gokonacha omoragia, onyora kwarengereirie** *(Ekero okonacha omoragia tiga ebe 'ng'a kwarengereirie):*
Before you decide to take over from a soloist in order to also lead a song, think first. (This is an advice to those who aspire to become leaders to first acquire the necessary skills.)

148. **Gokora buya ngosaria, Bogita!** *(Ogokora buya nogosaria, Bogita!):* So doing good is spoiling, Bogita! (This is a reaction from a benefactor who instead of being thanked is insulted.)

149. **Gokora ebinto chisese chikwanga** *(Ogokora ebinto chisese chiangete):*

Deeds abhorred by dogs. (This refers to an extremely immoral act of *obokayayu/obonyaka*, adultery.)

150. **Gosaba tikong'ana 'koiba** *(Ogosaba tikong'ana okoiba):* To ask for something is not synonymous to stealing. (A reference that encourages borrowing rather than stealing).

151. **Gosoka isiko ria'sanse** *(Ogosoka risiko ria'sanse):* To come out in broad day light. (A self-confessed wrong doer who is not remorseful).

152. **'Gosori ne'yamwabo 'mariga** *(Egosori ne'yamwabo amariga):*
 A joke is a relative of tears. (This is a warning to those who do dangerous jokes. Jests, like sweet meat, have often-sour sauce).

153. **Gotebigwa nigo, tikong'ana kwerorera** *(Ogotebibwa mbosa igo, tikoreng'aini okwerorera):*
Seeing is superior to being told. (You belief easily and readily when you witness an incidence by yourself compared to when it is narrated to you.)

154. **Gotiana mono, 'nkwagorera 'mbori mato** *(Ogotiana mono nabo konga okwagorera chimbori amato):*
Swearing too much is like plucking leaves from the branches of trees for goats to eat. Action speaks louder than words.)

155. **Gucha noira 'nsisi Mogonga n'okobua** *(Egucha, nokuma mono, Omogonga nokobuete):*
Gucha, despite your fame, Mogonga is stronger than you are. (The proverb teaches us that despite fame, popularity, and strength, one can be defeated by one who is weak and, perhaps, unpopular.)

Story-line: River Gucha is the longest river in Gusii; On the other hand, River Mogonga is a short but powerful tributary, which joins Gucha at its senile stage. River Mogonga thus pushes the waters of the tired Gucha with great force as if they were fighting, in which case Mogonga defeats the old Gucha.

156. **Gwankoreire 'nkorera bwa songoso, buna 'motembe ochia 'nting'ana** *(Gwankoreire bobe, bono nigo inkorera bwa songoso, buna omotembe ochire enting'ana):*
You have caused me to lament sorrowfully, sounding like a queen bee in a beehive.(This refers to a current incident, which reminds someone of his/her, previous problems. It is a situation in which someone adds insult to injury.)

I

157. **Inda 'ndongi, ereta 'muya, ereta 'morogi, ereta 'moibi** *(Enda n'endongi, nigo ekoreta omonto omuya, naende yarenta omorogi, naende yarenta omoibi):*
A womb is mysterious; it begets gentleman, wizards and thieves. (This refers to a womb, which brings forth children of different characters, attitudes and preferences. Some will become, carpenters, teachers while others will become thieves.)

158. **Ira "magoro make!** *(Ira amagoro amake):*
Shorten your pace/ slow down. (Advice to stop getting involved in a suspicious deal(s).

159. **Ira ng'ora buna 'ngobo ekoyia** *(Ira ng'ora buna engobo ekona koyia):*

Take your time and be patient like a burning skin garment. (This is an encouragement to young persons not to hurry into marital responsibilities. True love waits.)

160. **Irionya riatonya mairwana** *(Ririonya nigo rigotonya ekero okorwana):*
The feather falls during the combat. (One exhibits fierce emotions before he fights, but once he is confronted by the opponent he/she starts to show cowardice.)

161. **Ise 'moiseke tana kobugwa** *(Ise omoiseke tari kobugwa):*
The bride's father is usually in charge. (If a man loves a girl, he will perform all sorts of tasks in order to get the girl's hand. He will not argue with the prospective father in-law.)

162. **Ituko rimo 'ndioro, kwania abako, meremo tekoera** *(Rituko erimo n'erioro, kwania abako, emeremo teri koera):*
One day is like laziness; use it to visit in-laws; chores will never end. (This is encouragement to create time off to relax and even visit relatives.)

K

163. **Kaa 'mandegere name Getembe, k'otari na 'momura takoyaa** *(Kaa amandegere name Getembe, korende oyotari na omomura takoyaa):*

In future, mushrooms will sprout at Getembe (present-day Kisii town). However, those without "sons" will not harvest them.

Story-line: *These were prophetic utterances of the Gusii seer, Mzee Sakagwa, about the future wealth of Kisii town. Sons in this context refer to determined hardworking children especially those educated and are in prominent jobs.*

164. **Kabe nyamoyo 'muya buna 'mobarera 'ngobo** *(Kabe na omoyo omuya buna omobarera chingobo):*

Be as tolerant as the skin garment tailor.

Story-line: *Making a skin garment was a highly appreciated trade, which required patience, skill, perseverance and determination. Such people were admired for their high tolerance. They never charged much because they feared they might lose their skill, which was believed to have come from God.* (Also: **karie 'bike buna 'mobareri 'ngoba.**)

165. **Kae ababisa egeku, batekere morumbe, k'onye na 'mbura egotwa bironche bikwe 'mbeo** *(Kae ababisa egeku, obatekere omorumbe, naboigo onye embura egotwa ebironche bikwe embeo):*

May our enemies face starvation, may they stay in mist and may the rain pour and kill their sicklings. (This is a curse upon the enemies. It epitomizes the highest vengeance and bitterness of those whose wealth has been looted.)

166. **Kai 'ngochia ekebago 'ngoitere?; 'ng'ende kwebisa sasuri ya Monari** *(Ng'ai inkorusia ekebago ngoitere, erinde ing'ende kwebisa ase chisasuri chia'Monari):*
I wish I had a club with which to beat you up, and disappear to hide at the ravines of Monari. (Monari is one of the sub-clans of Kitutu. These people occupy a vast area of hills, ridges, caves, rivers and ravines. If someone hides there, it would be difficult to find him. This is a reference to enmity and refuge.)

167. *K*ai 'ngochia kobisa omotwe k'amakere atigare *(Ng'ayi ngochia kobisa omotwe erinde amakere oka atigare):*
I wish I had somewhere to bury my head, leaving only my torso exposed. (This is uttered when someone witnesses a bizarre incident. It is likened to the proverbial ostrich, which prefers to bury its head in the sand.)

167. **Kai okoria okobeka, k'enda yabeire eng'ara?** *(Ng'ai okoria kwabeka, ekiagera enda yao ere eng'ara?):*
Where does all the food you eat go? Your stomach is sunken and sagging. (A remark made towards a very skinny person who eats a lot.)

169. **Kang'o 'monibi   ki otari 'moganga?** *(Ing'orokie omonibi otari omoganga):*
Show me one business person who is not shrewd? (It is believed that in business one has to be cunning. This is used by business people as an excuse when found to be unscrupulous.)

170. **Kang'o 'morwoti ki otana 'bainyiambi?** *(Ing'orokie omorwoti otabwati abainyiambi):*
Show me one king who operates without buffoons? (These are those sycophants who are always near the king, more so to claim responsibility for his faults including his fouls.)

171. **Kare 'nkare, na rero 'ndero** *(Kare inkare, naboigo rero indero)*:
The ancient belongs to the ancient, and the modern belongs to the modern. (This is a reference that every age has its preferences. Things change with the time.)

172. **Karie, g'otigarerie bainani** *(Karie, ko otigarerie abagakare inani)*:
Eat a bit and reserve some for those still in the forest. (This is used to encourage savings for those who are not present including future generations.)

173. **Kaya 'nkaya kanga Mwango o'Matara** *(Omoiseke omuya, n'omuya, igo abwekaine Mwango o'Matara)*:
As beautiful as Mwango, daughter of Matara.
Story-line: *Miss Mwango, daughter of Matara, was once the most beautiful girl in Gusii land. She was small in stature but very charming and industrious.*

174. **Kebe keigwere bw'Omariba n'Omabeche omwabo** *(Ekebe nigo kere bw'Omariba na Omabeche omwabo)*:
A terrible curse has befallen the homestead of Omariba and his brother Mabeche. (This refers to a massacre done in the two homes by cattle rustlers, which stirred up the battle of Mogori in the early 1900.)

175. **Kebe 'nkia monyene** *(Ekebe ne kia omonyene)*:
The bad belongs to its owner. (One man's poison is another person's meat.)

176. **'Kee 'keyia 'nkeerwa** *(Ekee ekiyia nakio gekoerwa endagera)*:
A new *ekee* (plate) is preferred for serving food. (This refers

to a newly-married wife. She is given more attention than her older colleagues.)

177. **Keene 'keng'ese, 'mborimo** *(Ekeene kere itwania, noborimo kere):*
Half-truth is actually falsehood. (If one mixes truth with lies, the result is that he/she is lying.)

178. **'Keero kia 'monda 'nkeganga** *(Ekeero kia omonto omonda n'ekeganga):*
A rich man's offering/payment is stingy. (Used where a rich person does not pay debts in time. Often, rich people tend to ignore small debts, under pretext that they are too busy.)

179. **Kegocha 'ngiati 'nsiongo** *(Ekegocha nabo kegwata ensiongo):*
A trip or a small obstruction breaks the water pot. (This serves as caution to those people who like back-biting others.)

180. **Kenyenyi rimo nere ogoseeria 'baisia** *(Omonyenyi orimo nere ogoseria abaisia):*
The one slaughtering for the first time can be noticed by the way he chases away boys. (A reference to hosts who limit visitors due to inexperience.)

181. **'Keore 'kebese giachencha 'kende 'kiomo** *(Ekeore ekebese ekegochencha ekiamwabo kere ekiomo):*
A fresh skull laughs at a dry one. (A reference to those who mock others who have failed to succeed. Since each person has a weaknesses/shortcoming that is peculiar or unique to him/her. This warns us not to admonish them. We should not behave like a baboon which sees its colleague's behind but does not see its own.)

182.   **'Kia' nyabamo 'nyama yachiire 'rino** *(Eriomana ria abanto abamo nabo ringa buna enyama yachire erino):*

A quarrel between kinsmen is like a strand of meat stuck between the teeth. (This is used to warn people against interfering in affairs of people of the same blood).

183. **'Kiara kemo tikiana goita 'nda/nkoa** *(Ekiara ekemo tikeri goita enda gose enkoa):*

One finger has never killed a louse. (Unity is strength).

184. **Kiarinire omooko igoro** *(Nigo kerinete omooko igoro):*

It has climbed to the top of a fig tree. (What seems to be a small matter at first can turn out to be a complicated issue.)

185. **'Kina kia' 'mworo kiagamba 'miaka ebere mechinini ekagwa 'nse** *(Ekina kia omonto omworo nigo gekogamba emiaka ebere emetienyi yaera):*

A lazy man's case drags on for years and months. (The lawsuit of a fool never comes to an end. This is because they have no influence to help quicken the case.)

186. **Kiina obirore, okage 'mbinde** *(Kina nario orabirore tokaga 'mbinde):*

Grow up and you will learn the experience; so for now do not think you know! (Experience is the best teacher.)

187. **'Koboko 'nkwana gochia 'monwa birati** *(Okoboko tikori gochia omonwa birati):*

A hand does not get into the mouth empty. (This is an encouragement to engage in any work, which will provide some wages for food. Idle hands will not feed any mouth.)

188. **Kobwatia 'nchoke n'okoria 'boke, kobwatia 'ngi n'okorora 'bonyira** *(Okobwatia enchoke nokoria oboke, okobwatia engi nokorora obonyira):*

If you follow a bee you are likely to eat honey, but if you follow a house-fly, you are certain to encounter dung. (A good leader will deliver goodness while a bad one will deliver shame. Follow those likely to lead you to success).

189. **Kogita 'mochie 'nkomaria** *(Okogita omochie nokomaria):*

To keep a home intact one has to assume some behaviours among his offsprings. (An elder is not expected to question everything he sees at his home. He has to tolerate some bad habits especially displayed by his daughter-in-laws for the sake of peace and unity.)

190. **Ko'gotama ching'era, kwaumera chinchogu!** *(Ekero ogotama ching'era nigo ogochia kwaumera chinchogu!):*

You flee buffaloes only to encounter elephants!

(You can't flee from fate. You try to flee from one trouble you find yourself in another. From a frying pan to the fire. Face issues squarely instead of running away from them.)

191. **Ko'gosenkekigwa n'enyag'au, tang'oria, buna kwaereirwe nero yaererwe** *(Onye gokominyokigwa n'enyang'au, tama mono, ekiagera buna kwaereirwe nero yaereirwe):*

When a hyena is chasing you, keep on running, for the rate at which you are wearing out is the same rate the hyena is wearing out. (Never surrender to an enemy when you are in an advantaged position.)

192. **Kogoteeba Omokeira, n'Omogwasi bakoira** *(Ekero ogochora Omokeira, n'Omogwasi okoirwa):*

Once you advise one to go in for a bride from Bokeira clan, he will go in for a bride from Bogwasi clan. (This refers to one's choice in marriage. The parent's choice is not necessarily the best; hence not always obeyed. The son may proceed to marry a girl of his choice. The same is also used in tentative advice: "One man's meat is another's poison".)

193. **Koibora kobe 'nkwa 'nyoni etagotoma** *(Okoibora okore okobe nokw'enyoni etari gotoma):*
The worthless bearing is likened to that of a bird, which does not get assistance from its young ones. (This refers to an ungrateful child.)

194. **Koibora 'nkuya, gwakora 'mokungu 'monyaka 'nting'ana** *(Okoibora n'okuya, ekiagera kogokora omokungu omonyaka enting'ana):*
Bearing children is of great benefit; it transforms a "dirty" woman into a queen. (This refers to a woman who is despised, but who, having children who are educated and grown up and independent, start providing her with all necessities, making her look like a queen).

195. **Koirana 'matongo 'makoro** *(Okoirana ase amatongo amakoro):*
To return to the old homestead. (This refers to a polygamist, who eventually returns to his first wife).

196. **'Komiameria 'batwambu gwasinya koramokeria bayaye** *(Okomiamia amaiso ao ase abatwambu nigo orasinywe korora abayaye):*
Closing your eyes to the ugly ones will impair one from noticing the beautiful ones. (If one closes one's eyes to avoid seeing bad people, one will not know when the good ones are passing. Each case has its own merit. Generalization is not always beneficial.)

197. **K'oroche 'nkirete iga, naberekeirwe mana a'nchoke 'makinda tinkoyaria** *(Ekero oroche inkirete iga, nokoba naberekeirwe amana aye chinchoke amakinda tinkoyarria):*
The reason for my silence is that I have been forced to carry honey combs, which I do not desire to eat. (This has reference to being forced into situations in which one does not desire to be, even if they may be as good as honey. Example: when one is invited for a feast at a witch doctor's home; it is not an ordinary free home one would wish to be associated with.)

198. **Kororekia, nkwa 'ngi ekororekia isombe** *(Oyo'kogororekia nabo anga engi ekororekia risombe):*
To verify is just like a housefly verifying a dunghill. (There are situations which are obvious; it will be a waste of time trying to verify them.)

199. **Korusia 'mabi 'iiga** *(Okorusia amabi riiga):*
To remove faeces from the cooking stone. (It means to mature from childhood into boyhood. This is told a young boy who often sits next to his mother's cooking place.)

200. **Korusia echi'obonyenyi** *(Okorusia echi obonyenyi):*
To deduct the butcher's "tax". (This is in reference to assigning a butcher a specific piece of meat for his work, and indeed any payment made in appreciation of a job well done).

201. **Korusia esira y'emonyo** *(Okorusia esira ya emonyo):*
To pay an ant's debt. (This refers to payment to the circumciser. Ants feast on the discarded foreskins).

202. **Kurera abamura bairane, ng'ombe 'ntoki 'nse** *(Kura erinde abamura bairane, tibagenderera kobwatia chiombe, ekiagera chiombe nabo chigotoka nse):*
Advice the warriors to retreat, cattle belongs to the ground

(soil). (This is an advice for people to surrender instead of fueling up a revenge action. One may cultivate the soil and buy more cattle, instead of pursuing the armed rustlers who may terminate one's life.)

203. **Kwaora kwa 'monto 'monene, 'nkwoma; kwaora kwa 'mwana 'ntoro** *(Okwaora kwa omonto omonene, nokoba y'okwoma, okwaora kwa omwana omoke nokoba y'echitoro):* An adult's yawn signifies hunger; while a child's yawn signifies sleep.

M

204. **'Mabi 'makoro tana gotioka** *(Amabi amakoro tari gotioka):* Old faeces do not stink. (This refers to forgotten good deeds.) (Also in Kiswahili: *mavi ya kale hayanuki..*)

205. **Mogoroba yang'aina ankio** *(Magoroba igo ekong'aina aankio):* Evening cheats tomorrow. (A bad debtor gives false promises that he will pay his debt, which he doesn't.)

206. **'Maiko onsi 'mansa are** *(Amaiko onsi na amansa are):* Like gaps between the teeth, all places are the same. (One cannot escape problems by relocating, for similar problems are found there as well.)

207. **Makora imagoti n'ande acha** *(Amakora nigo akogota nayande aicha):* Generations pass and new ones come. (Every generation has its preference e.g. dance, fashion, style and regimes. You cannot rely on past glory.)

208. **Makweri 'makoro** *(Amakweri n'amakoro):* Death is an old thing. (This is uttered when one becomes
46

brave and decides to confront danger. It is also used to comfort the grieving.)

209. **Makweri a'mwana 'masenwa aiteka** *(Amakweri y'omwana na amasenwa ayare aitekire):*
The death of a child/youth is like spilt honey. (It is a big loss for a child/youth to die, since they possess potential which has not been tapped.)

210. **Manda 'maonchorerani, tokora bonde mache** *(Amanda nigo agoonchorerania, tokora bonde amache'):*
Wealth changes hands, do not water any down. (Even a poor person can become rich provided he works hard.)

211. **Mang'ana, 'mang'ana nyamoguto!** *(Amang'ana asokia amang'ana nde nyamoguto):*
Troubles bear other troubles, which resemble. (Reference to wonders that never cease.)

212. **Manwa tari 'mobe; Bundusi omwabo obeire ekemonchogo (ekeorochogo)** *(Manwa ere tari mobe; Bundusi omwabo obeire ekemonchogo):*
Manwa is not bad; it is his brother, Bundusi, who is chaotic. *Story-line: Two brothers used to quarrel over trivial matters for a long time, until both were assumed to be equally chaotic. However, with time people came to discover that one of them, Manwa, was a kind person, while his brother, Bundusi, was actually the one on the wrong.*

213. **Marwa aya mamuma, akagera 'ngaita ominto, 'ngacha gweitia aankio, k'omomera orwa omotwe** *(Amarwa aya na mamuma, nigo agerete ingaita oyominto, erinde ingacha gweitia aankio, ekero omomera orwete omotwe):*

Liquor is cursed, it made me kill my brother, only to regret in the morning, when sober. (Reference to influence of alcohol. It is an admonition to drink alcohol carefully.)

214. **Masanera 'moka 'momura notaramorora** *(Oyogosanera moka'momura, nokoba ere ataramorora):*
The excitement one has for one's daughter-in-law only exists before one sees her. (This refers to the eminent conflicts between parents and their daughters-in-law; never praise something you have not seen/experienced.)

215. **'Mbeba nyinge tichiana korema mong'anyi oike** *(Chimbeba chinyinge tichiri korema omong'anyi oike):*
Many rats do not succeed in digging a burrow. (Too many cooks spoil the broth.)

216. **'Mbura ng'ingi 'ng'eti** *(Embura ekoenga mono nigo egoeta):*
Dark heavy clouds do not bring rain. (A big threat is not necessarily going to result in harm. The wisdom here is that one should not be terrified by the size of the threats.)

217. **Mechie 'maburu!** *(Emechi na amaburu ere):*
Homesteads are synonymous to the initiator's seclusion chambers! (There are many hidden issues in various families.)

218. **'Mochobi tana korichanigwa** *(Omochobi tari korichanigwa):*
A slow but careful walker does not trip. (Slow but sure).

219. **'Moeti 'bisieri, 'monyori 'mara are iiga** *(Omonto ogoeta ebisieri, nigo aranyore amara are riiga):*
The one who frequents others' homes, is most likely to encounter intestines placed on the cooking stone. (This refers to a frequent visitor; he/she is likely to unearth disgusting weaknesses in others' families.)

220. **'Mogambi Gitogo chimori 'nyanya** *(Omogambi gitogo nigo chimori chikonyanya):*
While casing about Gitogo, calves have ravaged others" farms. (Refers some elders who concentrate on trivial cases, while bigger ones are left unattended.)
Story-line: A story is told about Gitogo, a hill frequented by fires during dry seasons. Elders could perpetually case on who caused the fire and in the process neglected other serious cases which involved cows ravaging crops.

221. **'Mogaso bara, 'nkonyenyere/'ngoitere ikongo ri'enyang'au** *(Omogaso baara, erinde inkonyenyere rikongo ria enyang'au).*
Sun, I beg you to shine; in return, I will slaughter for you an old hyena. (This refers to a persuasive appeal, which one knows is unlikely to be fulfilled. So in return he offers the very worst reward. It is used as a mockery against stubbornness.)

222. **'Mogeni tachi ikora, 'monyene orimanyire** *(Omogeni tari komanya ikora, n'omonyene omanyete):*
A visitor, although wise, does not know the details of a homestead; it is the owner who knows it all. (All new comers require induction.)

223. **'Mogesi tana gotura 'moragori** *(Omogesi tari gochia oboragori):*
A bachelor does not visit a diviner/seer. (Family problems normally start with marriage.)

224. **'Mogesi tana kogomia itinge!** *(Omogesi tari kogomia ritinge):*
A bachelor can not have a successful marriage with a divorcee. (A bachelor doesn't have enough experience in marriage to enable him know how to take care of a divorced

woman. A divorced woman will only exhaust his resources and eventually return to her former husband.)

225. **Mogusii oito n'Okong'o nyamenwa ebere** *(Omogusii oito nigo are Okong'o nyamenwa ebere):*
A Gusii person is "Okong'o," the double-tongued. (Okong'o is a person who is sly and supports opinions that only suits him, or opinions that can benefit him.)

226. **'Moibori omino 'nkerecha kere 'nyasi** *(Omoibori omino nekerecha kere enyasi):*
One's co-wife is a devil on the wall. (Co-wives have hidden jealousy and hatred for one another. They never see anything good in each other.)

227. **'Moigoto 'ntindo** *(Omoigoto nigo onga ogotinda):*
Too much satisfaction is tantamount to drunkeness. (When one is drunk, one becomes impaired and even inconsiderate to others' needs. People who have wealth are not conscious of other's problems.)

228. **'Moisia isuri ria 'ngoko, n'asambete egesa kio omogaka** *(Omoisia ne'risuri ri'engoko, nigo asambete egesa ki'omogaka):*
A boy is a chicken's burp/fart; he burnt the elder's hut. (This refers to mischief by the boys. They should be understood and always be guided.)

229. **'Moisia ogotebia ng'ina esegi, tiga atebie mogisangio** *(Omoisia ogotiema ng'ina esegi, tiga atieme omogisangio):* A boy who challenges his mother to a fight should instead do so to his contemporaries. (A mother deserves respect not challenges.)

230. **'Moita ('motema) keminyo tang'ana 'moimoka igo** *(oyogotema ekeminyo tang'ana oyore okoimoka bosa):*
The one who attains a fraction/portion is better off than one who gets nothing; better half a loaf than none.

231. **'Mokamosereti nere ogotwerwa mono** *(Omokungu onywomire n'omosereti nere ogotwerwa mono):*
It is the thatcher's wife whose hut leaks most. (Like most artisans, builders are anxious to make every cent out of their trade. In the process, they neglect their own homes; as result the roofs of their huts leak in rainy season.)

232. **Mokaya, oire enaigo kengeka/bogeka** *(Mokaya, oire enaigo gochia bogeka):*
Mokaya, direct the arrow to a wrong direction. (This is a back-biting remark meant to ill-advise an expert to divert from his workmanship.
Story-line: A story is told of Mokaya who was an expert in pricking a cow to get blood. His colleagues will come around to persuade him, by using the above proverb, to misdirect the arrow so that it kills the cow for meat instead of just pricking the blood-vain. The remarks were made through whistling or tongue twisting. Over a time, Mokaya was discovered and heavily fined.

233. **Mokinani tari obweetwe 'meni** *(Omokinani taiyio obweetwe emeni):*
No wrestler admits having been defeated. (All elders talk of having been heroes in their time; who did they all beat?)

234. **Mokombi boke, tana gokomba rimo** *(Omokombi oboke tari gokomba rimo):*
He who tastes (honey), does not do it once. (One who gives in to first temptation, will oftenly fall back to it.)

235. **'Mokoyone/kerindo agachia akamboa egesa n'orokini rw'eng'era** *(Omoko one agachia akamboa egesa amo n'orokini rw'eng'era):*

My brother-in-law is a friend indeed; he did fasten me securely with the belt of a buffalo skin. (This is a praise to a brother-in-law who is generous to his sisters-in-law, providing both food and clothing for them.)

236. **'Mokungu motakanwa mororere monanda buna agotanga nyamasio yaye** *(Omokungu omotakanwa omororere omonanda buna agotanga eng'ombe yaye):*

A widow's mettle is tested at the cow-shed when she tends to her stubborn cows. (In the absence of her husband, the widow's inexperience can be noticed.)

237 **'Mokungu moenenu (nyagetiara) moe oboremo bwa 'mbororwa agoaka abwata omotwe** *(Omokungu omoenenu moe oboremo bw'embororwa erinde gakorema obwata omotwe):*

An arrogant woman is allocated a hard ground to till. (An arrogant woman should be allocated a hard ground to till. This refers to disciplinary action taken to stem people's stubbornness/arrogance.)

238. **'Mokungu 'ngekori, tokomanya 'buya bwaye otaraikaransa inse** *(Omokungu nigo anga egekori, tokomanya buya bwaye ekero otaraikaransa inse):*

A wife is like one's bottom, you never appreciate its importance until when you sit down. (It is when one's wife goes away or deserts one that one realizes her importance.)

239. **'Mokungu tana gotomwa (gotura) 'sira** *(Omokungu tari gotomwa kobwatia sira):*

A woman is never sent to collect a debt. (It is believed that if a woman is sent to collect a debt she is likely to use a derogatory language when talking to the debtor, thus causing a quarrel.)

240. **'Mokungu tari kegori** *(Omokungu tabwati ekegori):*
A woman has no age group. (It is normal in the Abagusii community for a young woman to be married by an old man, but rarely vice versa.)

241. **'Mominchori imi tang'ana 'mosera ibu** *(Omominchori rimi tareng'aini oyore ogosera ribu):*
The one who endures the morning dew is incomparable to the one at the cinders. (One who wakes up early and braces the cold of morning dew will do well than one seated at the fireplace waiting for the dew to disappear. The early bird catches the worm.)

242. **'Mong'ainwa tari monene** *(Omong'ainwa tari ore monene):*
Any one, of any age, can be deceived. (Anyone, however wise or old, is prone to deceit.)

243. **'Monto 'mobe 'ngobo ya 'getondo** *(Omonto omobe nigo anga engobo y'egetondo):*
A bad person is likened to a shroud. (A bad person is never admired by anyone.)

244. **'Monto 'monene 'ndiogo** *(omonto omenene n'eriogo):*
An elderly person is "medicine". (Due to his experience he is capable of providing solutions to problems.)

245. **'Monto ona 'mosubati omwabo, agende gesere kia Nyamwamu, akunyorie mogoye ona kwoma, akore 'kericho na kwabeka** *(Omonto obwate omosubati omwabo, tiga agende egesera kia Nyamwamu, akunyorie omogoye ona kwoma, akore ekericho na ekiabeka):* Let one with a sister go to Nyamwamu's forest-land and pull out a "rope" (from tree bark) and be ready to tie it round an animal. (This refers to a man with many sisters. He better be ready to receive many animals (dowry) than he can take care of.)

246. **'Monto tana gosamba 'nyimbo ibere chibe** *(Omonto tari gosamba chinyimbo ibere chibe):* Nobody can burn (tattoo) two rods simultaneously and succeed. (Do one thing at a time. One cannot serve two masters.)

247. **'Monto tana gweitera** *(omonto tari gweitera):* A person never kills his own. (No matter how bad a child/ relative/friend is, being one of us, we have just to tolerate them). (Also: **'kebe 'nkiamonyene** *(Egento ekebe n'ekiomonyene)*)

54

248. **'Monwa 'muya orusia ng'ombe serere** *(Omonwa omuya nigo okorusia chiombe serere/ aare):*
A good "mouth" lures a cow from a far. (Sweet-talking during marriage negotiation can result to higher payment of dowry.)

249. **'Monua oreterera 'kogoro** *(omonua nigo okoreterera okogoro):*
The mouth causes trouble for the legs. (It is the mouth that hurls abuses and when trouble comes, the legs are the ones that help in running away. In the process the legs may slip and get injured, but the mouth that precipitated the trouble will be safe.)

250. **'Moragori 'mobe tachi 'nsembe yonde erabe** *(Omoragori n'omobe tari gotaka ensembe y'omonto onde erabe):*
An evil seer won't be happy to see one's cowrie shining. (This refers to jealousy.)

251. **'Moreera ise mono tana komoria 'mwando** *(Oyo okoreera ise mono tari koria omwando oye):*
The one who over-mourns his father does not inherit his properties. (A good person may not be commensurately rewarded; cf: the Biblical story of the Prodigal Son.).

252. **'Moria mono tari isankwa** *(Oyo koria mono tari koba isankwa):*
A glutton has little "skin". (Often a glutton hardly put on weight and little to show for all the food consumed.)

253 **'Moori a'ng'era tiyare gokwa n'eng'ina yabeire endongi** *(Emori y'eng'era tiyare gokwa, n'eng'ina ere endongi):*

The buffalo calf could not have died had its mother not gone roaming about. (This is a lamentation over a loss caused by a careless parent/guardian.)

254. **'Morogi ataragoita omogenki ogoitire** *(Omorogi ekero ataragoita nigo okonyora omogenki ogoitire):*
Before a witch kills you, a gossiper will do. (A gossiper is equally evil minded as a witch is. This is a warning to people to be wary of both.)

255.   *Mosacha kobwata 'nda 'nchara; 'mokungu kobwata 'nda 'mayianda (Omosacha okobwata enda nokoba enchara;, omokungu okobwata enda nokoba y'amayianda):*
A man to clutch his stomach is an indication of hunger; for a woman it is an indication of sorrow. (This is quoted when a man neglects his sick children and leaves the responsibility to the wife. A mother is usually more sensitive to children's problems.)

256. **'Mosacha irooka** *(Omosacha nigo anga omorooka):*
 A man is *irooka,* a tree that sprouts as soon as it is cut. (This refers to the fact that a person can still stand and prosper even after a great loss; this mostly used in business when one's properties have been lost through thuggery or arson.)

257. **'Mosae kengera 'mbusuro chiao, tichitaroka, chirusie bagaka kenuso 'mioro** *(Omosae okengere chimbusuro chiao, tichitaroka, erinde chirusie abagaka ebinuso chimioro):*

Young man guard your seeds lest they burst and in the process remove snuff from elders' noses. (This is a warning to the youth to take care of themselves, so as not to cause unnecessary worries to elders who are supposed to be relaxed with their sniff-tobacco.)

258. **'Mosacha 'mobaro (esabu) igo** *(Omosacha ore omobaro igo):*

A man is just by number. (This is a reference to a worthless man who leaves his responsibilities, e.g. taking care of his family to his relatives. He is a man by number; not value.)

259. **'Mosangami ikororo** *(Omosangami nigo anga rikororo):*

An uninvited guest is like a cough. (This refers to an uninvited guest who must always cough continuously to attract the attention of the host – that he has not been served.)

260. **'Mosomba n'onguru** *(Omosomba noyo bwe'chinguru):*

A servant must be energetic (strong). (If a servant is weak, he cannot work and earn a living given the demands. If one has chosen a career/work/job, let one work hard at it, and at no given time should one complain of its demands or hazardous conditions.)

261. **Mosuko 'moigoto, mosuko igwamo** *(Mosuko onyora imoigoto, mosuko onde onyora igwamo):*

Some days are of plenty; others of scarcity. (We need to understand that food can be abundant and at times scarce.)

262. **'Mosumi tana kweruseria** *(gwetaera) (Omosumi tari kwerusera):*

A borrower does not serve himself/herself (The one who is in need is not asked to take all they want.)

263. **'Moswaa 'nderema, itongo n'ogaya, itongo mwochochi** *(Omoswa nigo ore enderema, ritongo noo agaya, ne'ritongo omwochochi):*

A curse is like spinach; homestead is good; homestead is safe. (This is quoted when an elder is retracting a curse. This is a reconciliation of relatives.)

264. **'Motema 'tono tang'ana moirana birati** *(Oy'ogotema etono tareng'aini oyore okoirana birati):*

The one who picks a small mushroom is better off than one who returns empty-handed. (Better something than nothing at all. Better half a loaf than none.)

265. **'Motienyi okwa, oboka; monto akwa osira** *(Omotienyi nigo ogokwa naende oboka, korende omonto okwa osira pi):*

The moon "dies" and rises again, but man dies and goes for good. (This is in reference to death. The Kisii people believe that once a person dies, he reincarnates into an invisible spirit; which either brings blessings or curses depending on how he/she was handled when alive.)

266. **'Motomwa 'ndogoma are** *(Oyore ogotomwa nere okonyora orogoma):*

A messenger is the one who gets the injury; s/he faces the wrath of the recipient of the bad news delivered by the messenger. (It is fair for us to take the message as delivered and not to question or revenge on or fight the messenger.)

267. **'Motugi 'sese 'nyamoyo 'muya** *(oyore ogotuga esese n'oyore n'omoyo omuya):*
One who rears a dog is that one who is kind and tolerant. (This refers to someone who can accommodate dirty and/or lazy people.)

268. **'Motuguta mesweta (egutwa) maentenyi ng'a baiborwe** *(Timotuguta emesweta ekiagera amaentenyi naiborwe):*
Do not throw away the crown, great men shall be born. (A reference that clan people should preserve their current bad ruler, hoping a talented man will come up in future. This proverb is uttered during election campaigns.)

269. **'Muma 'muma, 'yariete omoro egatiga egete** *(Emuma n'emuma, ekiagera ekaria omoro egatiga egete):*
A curse remains a curse; it ate the matchet and spared the hilt. (A curse can kill the strongest if they are guilty and will spare the weak if they are innocent.)

270. **'Mwana 'nda, na ng'ina 'nda** *(Omwana nigo are n'enda, na ng'ina n'ere nare n'enda):*
A child has a stomach; its mother has a stomach. (Each person must fend for self in hard times; survival for the fittest.)

271. **'Mwana obande 'mamiria makendu** *(Omwana obande na amamiria amakendu):*
Someone's child is like cold mucus. (We always will prefer our own even if it is inferior/poor quality/ugly.)

272. **Mwa nyabaiseke 'bange, 'nkerandi getakwoma, k'obotakana tibogosira** *(Oyore n'abaiseke abange nabo anga ekerandi getari kwoma, korende obotakana tibori gosira):*

A home with many daughters will always have gourds full of milk, but yet end up being despised. (A reference that the girls will eventually get married, leaving the home deserted and despised for not having boys.)

N

273. **Na nyuma 'mborabe** *(Korwa nyuma nabo bokoraba):* It will shine later (with time). (This is an advice to be contended with what we have at the moment, with the hope that things will change for the better in future.)

274. **Nachia koria marore, nanya n'onde okoyaria** *(Nachire gokwana amang'ana amakong'u nanyorire nonde okoyakwana):* No sooner had I poured out my sorrows, than someone else also started his. (Be contented, for all of us have problems.)

275. **Nagenda magunkura chinda chioreka 'nsabo; nagenda tugutugu, chinda chioreka 'nsabo** *(Nabo inkogenda magunkura nabua; nakero kende nagenda tugutugu naende nabua):* I crawl on my stomach and succeed; I roll on my back and succeed too. (Remembrance of hard work, which eventually earns prosperity and respect.)

276. **Naikire, omokendo oika boruma** *(Nigo naikire buna omokendo ogoika boruma):* I have arrived where the tide settles into calmness. (This refers to a succesfull mission that has finally resulted into a comfortable life.)

277. **'Naki ogokenakena buna 'mbeba e'na itete?** *(Nigo ogokenakena buna embeba ere ne'ritete):*
Why are you restless/panicky like a rat carrying a millet husk? (A reference to someone who is nervous.)

278. **Nakobwatire chinderu naende nakoruseirie ekondo** *(Nigo nagosoroire naende nigo nagosikire mono):*
I have held you by the beard and saluted you. (This is an earnest request made to some respectable person for assistance.)

279. **Nakoeire gwasi ya 'ng'ombe n'abanto** *(Nigo nakoire egwasi ye'chiombe n' abanto):*
I proclaim to you the blessings of cattle and children. (This is a cardinal blessing pronounced by a father to a son during the initiation ceremony.)

280. **Nare gotama 'riansa, naumera mang'ang'ore** *(Nigo nare gotama oyore n'eriansa, korende naumera oyore mang'ang'ore):*
I flee from the one with a missing tooth and I meet the toothless one. (A reference to a woman who deserts a lazy husband and yet ends up with a drunkard; from a frying pan to the fire.)

281. **Nariete egetange n'euma** *(Nigo ariete egetange na euma):*
I "ate" both the railway track and the forked hoe. (This is a reference to living in extreme hardship.)

282. **'Nchera teri gotebia mogendi** *(Enchera teri gotebia oyore okogenda):*
A road does not tell a person what lies ahead. (A reference to misfortune and how no one can foresee it.)

283. **'Nchera ya bombera ngiya, nabo omo akorusia onde kiogoto riso** *(Enchera ya abanto babere n'engiya, ekiagera nabo oyomo akorusia oyonde ekiogoto eriso):*
A journey of two persons is safer; for one person may assist the other in removing a particle from the eye.

284. **'Nchogu 'yamete 'menge** *(Enchogu neya emete emenge):*
An elephant is one of many medicinal herbs. (An advice to try alternative treatment in order to be cured of a disease.)

285. **'Ndwari ya 'mobere obande, 'ngesomo ere (***Endwari ere ase omobere obande n'egesomo ere):*
A disease in another person's body is hidden. (One cannot feel another person's pain. None knows fully the weight of another's burden; it is the wearer of the shoe that knows where it pinches.)

286. **'Ngo tiyana kweibora n'ebisimba ekoibora** *(Engo teri kweibora n'ebisimba ekoibora):*
A leopard does not beget itself; it sometimes bears jackals. (This refers to successful parents who have spoilt children.)

287. **Nigo ogoseka buna otongoire okoria?** *(Nigo ogoseka buna omonto okoria ebi'atongoire?):*
Are you laughing like someone who has just harvested? (Happiness is found in those who have plenty. It is rare for the hungry to afford happiness.)

288. **Nigo oiranete nyuma buna egoti y'Obae (y'Obadia)** *(Nigo ore nyuma buna egoti y'Obae):*
You are as backward as Obae's (Obadia's) coat.
Story-line: Obae was a villager who was identified by his oversize coat that trailed behind him when drunk. The

meaning here is that in his drunken state, Obae was always behind news.

289. **Ninki esese yariete egakora 'bigoti?** *(Ninki esese yariete ekanoria ebigoti?)*:
What did the dog eat so as to posses that fat neck? (Be contended and eat what is available; that is the secret of fattening up.)

290. **Ng'a orotambe nduserie abanto baito rooche, orwane n'engegu rwaereire** *(Ing'ererie orotambe induserie abanto baminto korwa rooche, orwane nase engegu rwaereire)*:
Lend me a long belt to use in rescuing our drowning people; mine can't stretch beyond the bank. (This refers to an appeal for assistance to help one's relatives who are in difficulties.)

291. **'Nyeni chimo mwami nda** *(Chinyeni echimo nigo chikwamia enda)*: One type of vegetable tires the stomach. (Change of pasture brings forth fat calves.)

292. **'Ng'ina bosa okure Gesabakwa** *(Ng'ina bosa nigo akwerete Gesabakwa)*.
The mother of free things died at Gesabakwa.
Story-line: This is a reference to an elephant, which was killed at Gesabakwa (in the early 1950s) for all and sundry to enjoy free meat. People gathered there for over a week sharing, roasting, cooking and eating the free meat. It is used as a taunt to encourage hard work and discourage begging.

293. **'Ng'ombe tichiri 'muma, n'omochiurwa ogokwa; ko n'emechie togocha twarorera** *(Chiombe tichiri chimuma, nooria ourirwe ogokwa; korende n'emechie togocha twarorera)*:
Cattle stealing has no immediate curse, it is the owner who actually dies. However we come to notice the effects of it all in their future families.

Story-line: It is believed that the long-term effects of those people who were famous for cattle rustling is that they end up having no prosperity, while those who suffered frequent cattle raids produce very progressive individuals.

294. **'Ng'ombe yaito eiyerie ebwagi na ngoromomi k'abanchi baregana** *(Eng'ombe yaito ebiare omotienyi bw'ebwagi na yobw'engoromomi ekero abanchi bareganete):*
May our cow calf in the month of June or July when relatives gate-crash. (This is quoted during the famine season, when visitors can be a strain on a family.)

295. **'Ng'ombe yarenge yane yaroka 'monyenyi tata** *(Eng'ombe nonya yare eyane bono nigo ekoroka omonyenyi ng'a tata):*
The cow was initially mine, but now it addresses the butcher as its "father". (The butcher is more respected for supplying meat than the cow's owner.)
Story-line: Some people take over other's properties for their own gains while the owners are not recognized/ noticed, e.g. matatu conductors who take control of and show off with a vehicle they do not own.

296. **'Ngongo ibere** *(Chingongo nabo chire ibere):*
There are two distinct locations. (Always there are distinctions. Like in the rain season, one area may become too wet while the other remains dry.)

297. **'Nguba emo tekoira 'ng'ombe roche** *(Enguba eyemo teri koira chiombe roche):*
One shield is not enough to escort cattle to the river. (Refers to unity in a situation of communal threat, like protection against cattle rustlers.)

298. **'Nguru chia 'momura 'nchogu egwatia 'mbara** *(Chinguru chi'omomura nigo chinga enchogu egwatia chimbaara):*
A young man's energy is like an elephant splitting firewood. (Unless directed, a young man's energy may lead to self-destruction.)

299. **Nekiao orasarie** *(N'egento kiao orasarie):*
You will need to sacrifice what you own. (You can sell what you own to acquire something you don't have.)

300. **'Nkoonye rotwanetie, kaa 'ngokonye roichire** *(Inkonye rotwanetie, nainche mosuko ingokonye roichire):*
Lend me half; I will repay in full measure. (This refers to sharing and communal life.)

301. **Nonya n'engo, nere na 'ng'ina biara** *(Nonya n'engo nero nere na ng'ina biara):*
Even a leopard has a mother-in-law. (Even if you are a hero/famous/a celebrity/rich, you have someone who humbles or disarms you. This can be your wife, mother-in-law etc.)

302. **Noroga botuko, 'getutu 'nkere 'maiso** *(Noroga botuko, egetutu nkebwate amaiso):*
Even if you perform wizardry at night, the "bush has eyes". (Even the darkest secrets can be unearthed/revealed).

303. **Norore esese nyakemini** *(Nabo okorora esese nyakemini):*
You will see a tail-less dog. (This is deriding someone who acts foolishly.)

304. **'Ntakana ekebwata bobe egasira; 'ntakana ekebwata buya egachabumba** *(Entakana ekebwata bobe egasira; entakana ekebwata buya egachabumba):*

An orphan conducted himself badly and perished; another orphan conducted himself humbly and prospered. (One can prosper if one humbles oneself, and vise versa).

305. **'Ntindo ya 'bokima teng'ana 'ntindo ya 'marwa** *(ogotinda kw'obokima tikobwekaini ogotinda kw'amarwa):* Being "drunk" with ugali is more dangerous than being drunk with liquor. (One drunk with food is a fool.) (Related: *Moigoto, 'ntindo!*)

306. **'Ntone ng'ora, kogicha ontone buya** *(Ontone ng'ora, korende ontone buya):* Decorate me slowly, but, do it carefully/well. (Take your time and do a job well).

307. **Nyakenywera 'bande otana konywera gechuri mwaye, arore k'omomera ogooncha** *(Omonto okonywera mwabande, ere otari konywera nyomba mwaye erinde arore buna omomera ogooncha):* This man drinks in others' homes; he has never experienced the effect of yeast in his house. (This refers to a lazy man who is used to hand -outs).

308. **'Nyama 'nke yakoora 'bokima 'kee** *(Enyama enke yakora obokima ekee):* A small piece of meat finishes a heap of ugali in the straw-plate. (Do not despise a small thing/person. Remember the Biblical story of David and Goliath.)

309. **Nyambichu agesiena gokora nyongo, ko'moguba toigeti moiko buna marwa** *(Nyambichu nigo esienete gokora enyongo, korende omoguba toigeti omoiko buna amarwa):* Nyambichu, the imposter, set to make a pot but the furnace could not generate enough fire to complete the task. (Refers to stalled projects.)

310. **Nyamuya tegosareria oboko** *(Eng'ombe engiya tegera oboko bosareke):*
Don't let the beautiful cow spoil your marriage. (Don't spare something valuable if you can use it to achieve your goals).

311. **Nyang'era 'ndotungi ko n'emori yaye 'ndotungi** *(Eng'ombe ndotungi, n'emori yaye ndotungi):*
This black cow is an exact copy of its calf. (Like father like son).

312. **Nyangore 'mang'eng'a, akang'eng'a chia Mosiori gachigocha 'nka** *(Nyaribari nigo bare amang'eng'a nigo bang'eng'ete chiombe chia Mosiori gachigocha inka):*
Nyangore is sly; he once taxed Mosiori's cows when they were coming home.
Story-line: A story is told of how Nyangore, the father of the present Nyaribari clan, trained his sons as community warriors against cattle rustlers. They reimbursed their efforts with a cow from the cattle they recovered. Afterwards when there was no incident of cattle rustling, they continued taxing the dowry-cattle being passed through their place.)

(NB: This is also one of the satires that are spoken on every other Kisii clan. They are not necessarily true but are meant to be used with a light touch to evoke fun and laughter. Most clans have such satires, some are mentioned in this book.)

313. **'Nyantacho teri 'mokamo** *(Ng'ombe ekoruta chintacho nonya mabere tebwati):*
A cow, which kicks a lot, doesn't produces much milk. (A reference that a poor person is full of complaints, especially when requested for a donation.)

314. **Nyariansa, tonyeria amarua arore** *(Omonto ore n'eriansa tiga atonyeri amarwa arore):*

You who has a missing tooth, add yeast to the liquor to ferment it. (This is a remark meant to ridicule a boasting ugly person.)

315. **Nyoni e'na mage teri konora, n'ena magena ekonora** *(Enyoni ebwate amage teri konora, ney'ebwate amagena ekonora):.*
The bird with chicks doesn't fatten, it is the one with eggs that fattens. (This refers to a couple bringing-up children, in comparison to those who are newly- married and have not had children.)

O

316. **Obogotu 'ngesanko 'ngokina kore okuya, tangori ng'irane bwana** *(Obogotu nigo bore egesanko, ogokina nakwo kore okuya, ng'aki ndakore ng'irane obwana!):*
Old age is a crust; it is youth that is good. I wish I could go back and be young. (This is a lamentation old people. "Youth is a blunder, manhood a struggle and old age a regret.")

317. **Ochie kare buna e'Manga n'Esameta, na oibore n'egeting'e keibore** *(Ochie kare buna e'Manga amo n'Esameta, naende oibore goika egetinge keibore):*
May you sustain long life like Manga ridge and Sameta hill; may you bear children till the anklet bears too. (This is a blessing pronounced by a grandmother/father to a bride just before the departure to her husband.)

318. **Ogasusu mogeni otiokire aiga** *(Egesusu ekegeni giatiokire aiga):*
A smell of a visiting hare has been sensed around. (A remark especially meant to welcome a young visitor.)

319. **Ogoaaka e'koko** *(Okomanyia abanto amang'ana abeire)*:
To make a silent alarm. (To alert people of stolen properties, especially when a suspect is around. To allude to a thief when he/she is around.)

312. **Ogoakera amache oroe** *(okorua birati)*:
To slap water. (An unsuccessful mission.)

321. **Ogosiara ororenda** *(okworokia obotindi)*:
To display fury. (An act of spreading unwarranted fear, especially from an irresponsible elder.)

322. **Ogosaria obonyansi** *(Ogokwa gotabwenereti)*:
To spoil the grass/lawn. (A reference to the deceased, especially to the one who caused his own death through reckless living.)

323. **Ogosimora obonyansi/emurwa** *(Ogosorora mono mono)*:
To uproot grass. (An act of begging for mercy as a last resort. Such a person should be forgiven, whatever the circumstances.)

324. **Ogotarera (ogotamera) emete**:
To cling or hold onto plants. (Looking for a scapegoat, even when one is out-rightly guilty.)

325. **Ogusero akang'aina Otondo, Otondo agatonda chinsoti** *(Omogusero nigo ang'ainete Omotondo, omotondo agatonda chinsoti)*:
Ogusero clan misadvised Botondo clan; Botondo ended up hosting vultures.
Story-line: A story is told about the exodus from the Kano

plains. Thinking that Ogusero had crossed a deep river, the people from Botondo clan tried to do the same, but all drowned and the vultures had a feast.)

326. **Ogwatia (ogoaka) enangi** *(Okogosa oyosaririe):*
An appeal to declare innocence. (Used to dare someone who had stolen).

327. **Okobaranya ontune** *(Okonyenyera abanto enyama):*
To dish out beef. (Sharing out free meat).

328. **Okoegwa eng'ae buna eng'uko ere ase orobago** *(ogochandwa):*
To cause one's anxiety like a mole at the hedge. (To cause trouble, especially of settlement.)

329. **Okogenda enyoni n'omoengwe** *(Okobuta mono):*
To journey like the bird and the stick. (This proverb is used to refer to a situation where one is sent on errand but takes an inordinate amount of time to report back.)

330. **Okomena amaroba** *(ogotiana bobe):*
To lick soil. (To fervently deny wrongdoing.)

331. **Okoreirwe enyangi etari na kiore** *(Okonyora obokong'u obonene):*
He has been wedded without a wedding crown. (A reference to a tragedy.)

332 **Okoria oborominta (***Ogokana naende gokorete bobe):*
To talk venomously. (A reference to a killer who vains innocence.)

333. **Okoria emerare** *(okorondoria amang'ana atari na eng'echo):*

To eat stories. (This refers to someone who beats about the bush when called upon to pay a debt.)

334. **Okoria emuru** *(Ogosemania ekero ki'emechando):*
To talk of sorrow. (This is a quiet discussion by kinsmen during the death of a relative meant to find the way forward for the widow and the family.)

335. **Okoria esita** *(Ogwetogia):*
To act a hero. (A mock-war like action staged by a hero in order to encourage others.)

336. **Okoria o'mobogani bobe!** *(Okonyakaa/ ogokayaya):*
To eat a lot in hotels! (A reference to an amorous person. Hotels are believed to be the places where illicit love affairs take place.)

337. **Okweanya (okweota) mono 'ngekobo** *(Ogwetogia mono n'ase egekobo kore):*
To boast too much is only on the lips. (This refers to those who talk too much and act less.)

338. **Omobisa bw'etago n'embiro** *(Omobisa bw'etago amo n'embiro):*
An enemy of the indigo and the soot. (Two enemies who are irreconcilable.)

339. **Omochie o'tata okona gosoka abaya n'abanchi ba 'romeme** *(Oyo n'omochie o'tata okona gosoka abanto abaya na abanchi b'oromeme):*
My father's home brings forth beautiful ones and the lovers of the tongue/sweet talkers. (This is a reference to a person who has brought up a successful family with handsome sons and beautiful daughters.)

340. **Omogaso n'omuya mbuna otameti** *(Omogaso nabo ore omuya, korende notari kwamia):*
Although the sun is good, it does not support growth of crops. (People enjoy freely when there is no rain; yet without rain there would be no crops.)

341. **Omogwa 'roswa** *(Omonto ogwete roswa):*
The one who behaves like the devil. (This is a rebuke meant for a very evil-minded person, for example, a person who tends to poison food at a wedding party to destroy life.)

342. **Omoiseke ore sobo 'nsigiti etaratwata** *(Omoiseke kare sobo nigo are buna esigiti etarabiara):*
An unmarried girl is likened to an ewe that has not given birth. (An unmarried girl is beautiful and confident since she has no worries brought by married life.)

343. **Omoiseke omonyambu 'imbe 'monto o'are aganyete**
(Omoiseke oyore obwate chimbwa chimbe n'omonto okare aare aganyete):
A badly-behaved girl is usually married to people from afar. (People from afar do not know much of her background.)

344. **Omoiseke esang'onde (omonyamobwato) omonyene emori n'amorooche** *(Omoiseke omobariri, oyogochi komonywoma namoroche):*
A beautiful girl (with huge thighs) has been noticed by the calf owner. The proverb is saying that a beautiful girl is easily noticed by suitors.)

345. **Omoisia omobe n'otakoriera 'nchoke 'morero** *(Omoisia omobe noria otari koriera chinchoke omorero):*
An expert does not use fire in harvesting honey. (A reference to a brave man who endures pain, but eventually succeeds.)

346. **Omokungu omobe 'nsagasaga ekobuga buna 'maemba a 'nkongo** *(Omokungu omobe nigo anga buna esagasaga ekobuga buna amaemba abongirwe):*
A badly-behaved woman is likened to the rubbing together of rotten millet; eaten by weavils. (When rotten millet is being ground, it produces an irritating sound.)

347. **Omokungu omweanyi, motarere 'toigo** *(Omokungu omwerori motarere ekero ki'embura):*
Visit a proud woman during the rainy season. (It is only an industrious woman who affords firewood; hence serve good meals during all seasons, including the wet season.)

348. **Omomenyi oboko n'onga Gisore** *(Omonto okomenya oboko noy'ogwete Gisore):*
If one has to reside at his in-laws, he must emulate Gisore.

Story-line: A story is told of a man called Gisore who decided to stay with his in-laws because he was an orphan. He was very humble, good natured and industrious. Everyone liked him, and regarded him as one of theirs. He even married and brought up a family and acquired property. Eventually, when he left everyone missed him).

349. **Omomura kare sobo ne rirubi nyamong'ento**
(Omomura ore sobo nigo anga rirubi ribwate omong'ento):
A young man at his home is likened to a king cobra. (He is proud and even provocative.)

350. **Omonibi 'ng'ombe, 'ngoko agochakera** *(Omonto ogocha oniba eng'ombe n'engoko anibete ritang'ani):*
To own a cow, one must first have owned a hen. (One cannot realistically acquire wealth overnight; he must start from a humble beginning then grow to become rich.)

351. **Omonwa oriete obori, noro okoboria ninki ndabusure?** *(Omonwa oriete obori naende noro okoboria embusuro):*
The mouth that ate millet seeds is the same one that asks "where do I get seeds for planting?" (Do not consume everything; preserve some for the future.)

352. **Omorigia ekong'a (empere/ebitina) arigie n'ekerubo ekegare aterere** *(Omonto ogochegia ekong'a boigo tiga arigie ekerubo ekegare ase agoterera):*
The crane bird's hunter should also have a vast plain land to sing on. (A crane bird with chicks is very ferocious; it may gouge the hunter's eyes and he starts wailing, referred to as singing. So before one embarks on a risky venture, let him think twice.)

353. **Omoriri buna enda y'amabere** *(Omonto omoriri buna enda y'amabere):*
As foolish as the stomach full of milk. (When one feeds on sour milk he usually falls asleep, even during the day.)

354. **Omoyio (omoro) n'otebete ng'a omoisia oyio 'mbise** *(Omoyio ogateba ng'a omoisia oyio ogocha mbise):*
The sword (machete) cried out, "there comes the lad, hide me." (Mischievous lads love playing around with dangerous objects, or weapons, e.g. sharp swords. Because of their inexperience they are not supposed to be left in possession of such weapons.)

355. **Omwana 'natebetie ng'ina buna "tongia ekiage bono naigotire."** *(Omwana agatebia ng'ina buna "samba ekiage ekiagera naigotire"):*
A child told its mother: "Mom, you may now burn the granary since I have had enough food." (This refers to people who, following temporary satisfaction, destroy what should be useful in the future.)

356. **Omwetweki 'nko bogeka** *(Omokungu oyogwetweka chinko bogeka):*
The one who carries a bundle of firewood across the head. (A bundle of firewood is normally placed on the head facing in front. If placed across the head, it inconveniences others walking along or past the one carrying the bundle. So a woman who carries her's across the head is not only considered rude but also wicked. Hence the saying is used as a reprimand for obstinate women.)

357. **Ona 'gesero tana koborwa 'boraro** *(Oyore n'egesero kiaye tari koborwa are akorara):*
The one who possesses a sleeping hide/mat, will not lack

a sleeping place. (Refers to a person who has relevant or needed qualifications for a certain job.)

358. **Ona 'semi semia o'mino** *(Oyore n'echisemi tiga asemie oy'omwabo):*
Let the wise person share his wisdom with others. (Share your ideas/opinions/advice with others.)

359. **Onwong'a abunigwa kiaye** *(Onwong'a nigo akobunigwa egento kere ekiaye):*
Onuong'a is condemned for his own property. (This refers to jealousy and envy towards the poor who are progressing).

360. **Orang'o mana koria 'boko anakwangwa, nairanere Nyachere** *(Ekero Orang'o akoboria oboko erinde bwangwa rirorio nairanere Nyachere):*
As Orango gets disappointed with his marriage proposals, he will eventually revert to Miss Nyachere. This proverb is used as a warning to "macho-men" who misuse girls and leave them for others.
Story-line: A story is told about Orang'o who married Nyachere, whom he soon jilted. He proposed to many other girls who rejected him. He eventually came back to Nyachere.

361. **Ore agaya oteeba 'nde abe, na ore abe oteeba 'nde agaya** *(Omonto ore ase agaya nigo agoteeba buna nigo are ase abe, oyo ore ase abe ere oteeba nigo are ase agaya):*
One who is in a comfortable position complains of miseries, while one in a bad position says he is in a happy position. (It is hard to understand what makes people happy. Each one defines his/her own life using his/her own measure.)

362. **Otabwati o'mwabo ogwa/obwata moraa 'mwomo, obwate omwabo obwatwa 'koboko ocha 'ka** *(Omonto*

otabwati oyomwabo nigo akowa omoraa omwomo, korende
oyo obwate oyomwabo nigo akobwatwa okoboko oicha inka):
The one without a kinsman will fall on dry wood; the one
with his kinsman will be directed to safety. (A reference to
brotherhood and unity. Sometimes refers to nepotism.)

363. **Otwori nyangena ime, abatabori tibari 'boba** *(Oyo*
Otwori nigo akobugeria engoma rigena ime, kworokia buna
abatabori tibari boba):
Otwori,the horn man/horn blower, blows his horn in the
caves, a sign that Botabori clansmen are never cowards.
Story-line: Abatabori is a clan in Gusii whose warriors were
often used as mercenaries in inter-ethnic wars. As a result,
they are spread along all sides of the other main clans. They
were renowned for using powerful sounding horns through
caves to alert warriors and instill fear on the enemies.

364. **Oyo oriete ebi'onkong'a** *(Omonto omokoro mono):*
The one who ate the "anthrax meat."
Story-line: A story is told of a time when famine struck
Gusiiland. Anthrax killed cattle and the few that were left
were slaughtered before they also could die. The slaughtered
animals were smoked and kept for consumption. Such meat
was referred to as Onkong'a. Many people died and those
who survived had a tale to tell many years later. Hence, the
survivors were referred to as "of the age of Onkong'a". This
was probably between 1890 and 1900.

365. **Oy'onywomete 'mbirero are, n'oyo otanywometi**
nere 'mbirero are *(Omonto onywomete nigo akorera, nabo*
igo noria otaranywoma nere nigo akorera):
The married man is lamenting; the unmarried one is also
lamenting. (The one married is nagged by his wife; while the
unmarried is not respected.)

R

366. Rero 'ndero ritimbo riagonkirie Nyamareria Ongoro
(Rero nario rituko ritimbo riagonkirie):
Today is the day when a beetle has sucked! (It is doom's day. A reference to a very tough competition. A difficult and rare experience.)

367. Rigwa 'ndiaitete Omomanyi *(Rigwa nigo riaitete omomaasai):*
A thorn killed a Masai.
Story-line: A story is told how a Maasai, feeling severe pain on his foot, searched and found a very small thorn in his foot. On realizing how tiny it was, he decided to return it as a sign of bravery. Later it proved poisonous and killed him. Never take anything for granted, even a small thing can turn fatal.

368. Rikongo tiriana kwebeka 'ngori *(Nonya n'engombe ere rikongo tiyana kwebweka engori):*
Even an old cow has never tied itself for slaughter. (It is unheard of for a girl in the Abagusii community to propose to a man. The girl waits for a man to propose and not her.)

369. Riomana ria 'mokungu tiriana koirwa 'tureti *(Eriomana ri'omokungu tiriri koirwa kegambero):*
A woman's quarrel is never presented before the elders.
Story-line: Women are believed to be quarrelsome in nature. So if you present a case concerning your wife to the elders, then be prepared to appear before them every day throughout your life, since she will always make a mistake.

370. **Risimba ria magona mabe riegosia 'mbeba koria** *(Egesimba ekenene gekogona bobe nigo gekogera chimbeba chiegosa erio tigechiikera gechirie):*
The wild cat that snores loudly will scare away rats and miss his meal. (A reference to a noisy, thankless person, who is shunned in the process.)

371. **Ritinge 'ndia 'mochie 'mogare** *(Ritinge nigo rire erio omochie omogare):*
 A divorcee belongs to a large home. (A reference that the divorcee will always be planning to assert herself in the new home; she needs many people some to relate with and others to censure her manoeuvres.)

372. **Rogena ruya, rwaborwa 'nsio 'ngiya** *(Orogena oruya nigo rokoborwa ensio engiya):*
A fine grindstone lacks a good milling stone. (A reference to those good women who fall in the hands of lazy husbands and vice versa.)

373. **Rogoro 'ndwa ng'oi na biiri** *(Rogoro/aare nigo ere y'eching'oi n'ebiiri):*
Foreign land is full of frustrations and looters. (Investments done in foreign lands may be lost or confisticated due to prejudices.)

374. **Rosuku 'romo 'ndwana kobuga** *(Orosuku oromo tirori kobuga):*
One string will never make music. (Be in a team so as to be recognized and to derive group benefits. Unity is strength.)

S

375. **Samberebere 'nyama 'ngetinya** *(Okoebereria egere osabere enyama nigo okorasaba egentinya):*
The formula for begging for meat is first to request for fat.
Story-line: In the olden days, among other uses, fat was used to varnish a walking stick. However, a butcher, in most cases found it embarrassing to give a friend fat alone. He could therefore cut some meat and hand it along with fat. This is used to justify generosity even in business.

376. **'Semi tiching'ana 'nguru** *(Chisemi tichireng'aini chinguru):*
Wisdom is superior to physical strength. (Strategy/technique is superior to brute force.)

377. **Seito 'nseito, ase abamura bakwanga abagaka bagecha emiobo** *(Seito nao aria abamura bakwanga, abagaka bagecha emiobo):*
Our home is unique; the young men refuse to build so the old men cut poles. (The present generation of young men rebel and vacate home for greener pastures, leaving the old to fend themselves.)

378. **Seria 'ngoncho korwa 'kenagwa teira chingero Bogirango.** *(Seria engoncho korwa ekenagwa erio teira chingero Bogirango):*
Chase the parrot from the hedgerow so that it does not tap and carry our song-tunes to Bogirango. (A warning to be a ware of spies in meetings.)

379. **'Sira 'ng'iri 'moiseke** *(Esira nabo ekoira omoiseke):*
A bride is married on debt. (This refers to dowry, which is normally paid in installments.)

380. **Sira nkegonkorio, tosabera mosira roku** *(Esira nigo ere ekegonkorio, tosabera omosira amakweri):*
A debt is like pieces of broken pot, do not curse your debtor. (A debt like broken pieces of a pot never grows old. It will be paid even in the far future, provided both parties are living.)

T

381. **Tanga koibora 'nkorerere** *(Tang'ana koibora erinde inkorerere):*
Be the first to give birth so that I may be your maid. (This is a discontent remark between young women. It is meant to humble a proud newly married woman who despises others.)

382. **Tang'eri tata na baba 'ngesire, bakogota nimbaraga, nakonya nambura egotwa mbaragere gesona** *(Tangori tata na baba n'egesire bare, erinde bakogota nabaraga, nekero embura egotwa nabaragera gesona):*
I wish my father and mother were axes so that I would smelt them back when they age, and if rain interferes, I continue working on them at the verandah.
Story-line: A lamenting remark made by daughters mourning their beloved parents. Axes are renewed by hammering/ melting them into shape and then sharpening.

383. **Tichiana kogiterwa chitaigoreiri** *(Chiombe tichiana kogiterwa chitaratemwa koibwa):*
You never fortify your *boma* before an attempt of cattle raids. (Security is taken for granted till attempted burglary.)

384. **Tiga ribe itimo 'mbaba** *(Okomochia/ogoutia):*
Let it be the spear that flies over. (This is a remark made when a friend narrowly escape a bad accident.)

385. **Timoita 'gesimba gioka, ita na 'ngoko nero, 'nki yachiete korigia 'nani gati?** *(Timoita egesimba gioka, mwaita ne engoko nero, ninki yachiete korigia rinani gati?):*
Do not condemn the jackal, alone, condemn also the hen, for foolishly venturing into the forest. (Diligent care should be taken by the weak to avoid loitering into the enemy's territory.)

386. **Timoita 'ntakana, tiga echabumbe ko gicha techia koiba** *(Timoita entakana, tiga echabumbe ko gicha techia koiba):*
Do not torment an orphan, let him grow-up, provided he does not steal. (Take care of the weak or vulnerable or the disadvantaged.)

387. **Timotama! Eyio n'Okione yeonchoire korwa ribencho** *(Timotama! Abwo n'Abakione beonchoire bakorwa ribencho ime):*
Do not flee, these are our own warriors disguised, emerging from the leeds. (In the old days, warriors could play a trick by dressing and even speaking like enemies.)

388. **Timorora chigocha mochisekere, 'menuko chigosora** *(Timorora chiombe chigotemwa gocha mochisekere, n'emenuko chigosora):*
Do not rejoice at the acquired wealth, because it has taken pain and death to acquire it. (Some people have gotten their wealth through dangerous means; they should be sympathized with, rather than being cheered up.)

389. **Tinkoria bwa mosacha, 'mbwa 'mokungu 'ndarie** *(Tinkoria bokima bw'omosacha, nobw'omokungu indarie):*
I shall never eat what belongs to a man; I may only eat what belongs to a woman. (This was the perceived cry of a warthog when it was seriously wounded by a farmer. A thief will prefer a weaker victim.)

390. **Tiyana gokwa etaberegeti 'getondo** *(Teri gokwa etaberegeti egetondo):*
It has never died without dragging a corpse with it.
Story-line: Abagusii believe there is no calamity without a cause. In the olden days, the Gusii people believed that all deaths had a cause: it could be an act of witchcraft, poisoning, curse, spell or ancestors' annoyance.

391. **Tiyana gotwa etagukureti** *(Mbura teri gotwa etagukureti):*
It has never rained without first thundering. (Every occurrence has a pre-cursor/forerunner.)

392. **Toaka 'moigwa, noigusigwe okoboko** *(Toaka omoigwa nigo oraigusiwe okoboko):*
Do not beat up a nephew, you will be infected by Parkinsonism. (Nephews are tenderly cared for by uncles. It is a taboo to beat them up. Their respect stems out of the love for one's sister.)

393. **Tokaga imoneke otari igwa** *(Tobaisa gokagera buna oyo n'omoneke otari rigwa):*
Do not liken this to the spinach stem which is thornless. (Some situations are more dangerous than they seem to be on the surface.)

394. **Tonaria 'mogeni ('mogere) 'borere, onarire inse** *(Tonaria omogeni oborere, ere onarire inse):*
Do not allow a stranger to be accustomed to sharing your bed; s/he should be content with sleeping on the floor. (Like the story of the Arab and the camel, the stranger may eventually topple the owner and take over control of his affairs. "Indulgence breeds contempt.")

395. **Toira 'ngoro a'nchoka kiara** *(Tosoyia engoro y'eng'iti engenda inse ekiara):*
Do not poke your finger into a snake's hole. (Do not rattle a snake. An advice to keep off dangerous situations.)

396. **Toita iso, mambia 'mbokie onyuome** *(Toita iso, ekiagera mambia nabo egoika erinde onyuome):*
Do not kill your father, tomorrow shall come and you will marry; it is important to be patient.
Story-line: A story is told of a young man who killed his father because he postponed his wedding date. He ended up missing both the father and the bride.

397. **Toitera 'moisia 'nkundi, n'egesaku ogosiria** *(Toaka omoisia enkundi ekiagera ekio n'egesaku ogosiria):*
Do not punch a lad; that could extinguish a clan.   (In the process of beating up a boy, you may injure his genitals and he will become impotent. You would have terminated his ability to bear children and extinguished the family lineage.)

398. **Tokaga 'nchi'Omata chikoria 'bara a'mogere** *(Tokaga echi n'echi'Omata chikoria ebara y'omogere):*
Do not liken my case to that of Omata's goats which freely licks the trader's salt.
Story-line: A story is told of a man called Omata who used to release his goats to the market to lick traders' salt and other items. He knew the traders could not take action since they were visitors in the area. Now, at a neigbhouring market, another man started behaving like Omata. However, the traders were locals; they confiscated the goats and heavily fined him.

399. **Tokonyara noita Oreri na mwaye** *(Tokonyara noita Oreri na mokaye):*
You cannot succeed even if you killed both Oreri and his

wife. (Some situations are better left alone. It may be harmful to try changing them.)

400. **Tonia ase okorwa** *(Tosaria ase okorwa):*
Do not defecate where you have been dwelling.
Story-line: A story is told of man, on leaving his employer's quarter to his home, decided to spoil it and even defecated in it. He further instructed both his wives and children to do the same. Unfortunately, on that day he failed to get a bus going to his home. It started raining. He and his family were forced to go back, sweep the feaces, and repair the doors and windows to stay in for the night.
(Also: **Tonia ase kwaigamire!:** do not defecate where you have sheltered.)

401. **Tonkoria etichi y'okirimiti** *(Tonkoria emeremo ya okirimiti):*
Do not compel me to work on agreements.
Story-line: In the colonial days, locals used to sign employment agreements without understanding the contents. Some of these agreements had hidden terms meant to exploit them. Hence, a reference to any deals with hidden agenda.

402. **Toruta ritimo gochia 'nyomba** *(Tobaisa koruta ritimo gochia enyomba ime):*
Do not throw a spear towards the (your) house. (A warning not to cause trouble to the innocent kinsmen.)

403. **Totiana maseta, tiana masetoka** *(Totiana gokogenda goseta, tiana ekero kwairanire):*
Do not swear when setting off, swear when returning. (Play champion after success not before.)

404. **Totogia 'moiseke 'kieni, motogie 'mwana** *(Totogia omoiseke ekieni, motogie okoba aiboire omwana):*
Do not praise a woman because of her beauty; praise her because of her ability to bear children. (The crown of a woman is not her beauty but her children.)

405. **Totogia momura 'kieni, motogie 'nkoro** *(Totogia omomura ekieni, motogie enkoro okoba agokora amaya):*
Do not praise a man on account of his handsomeness, praise his heart. (That is the man's generosity.)

406. **Tureti etari 'kiina, 'mbamura etabwati** *(Ekenyoro getari n'ebina, na abamura bataiyo):*
A locality without cases has no young men. (A reference that youth compete with one another and disputes are inevitable, requiring resolution.)

407. **Twoni ibere tichiana koiyekerwa 'getega kemo** *(Chitwoni ibere tichiana koiyekerwa egetega ekemo chiyie):*
No one has ever successfully cooked two cocks in one pot. (A reference that each house must have only one leader. Figuratively, no wife should ever be shared by two men. It is a sacrilege.)

Y

408. **'Yare gokia yanga 'matiebo oyesaririe** *(Rituko anga riakia buya embura yarisaririe):*
It could have been a fine day, but rain has spoiled it. (Refers to a suddern down pour of rain especially in the morning hours, resulting to a bad day.)

409. **'Ya bobisa teri maira** *(Emechando ya ababisa teri kororerwa amabera):*

One that belongs to an enemy has no pus. (A reference that the problems of an enemy, however severe, are never noticed; nor should they be of concern.)

410. **Yachiire 'monwa omakera** *(Yarimeire):*
It has gone through the mouth of no return! (A reference to an irreversible action.)

411. **Yamerire ekuri** *(Atiekire koera):*
It has swallowed a thighbone. (It has come to an end. It is irreversible.)

412. **Ya'mokungu teri keu!** *(Eng'ombe y'omokungu teri gotwara ekeu!):*
The slaughtered cow that belongs to a woman has no provision for the belly meat! (When the butcher has completed his work, he normally cuts any portion of the meat for tasting purposes. However, if the cow belongs to a woman, she will not accept any part to be cut for tasting. This shows how strict women are with their properties.)

413. **Yarinire omooko** *(Yasinyire):*
It has climbed the fig tree. (The task has become impossible to achieve.)

414. **Yachiete sagare, koirana 'nkeribe** *(Eng'ombe yasaragetigwe bono yairanire k'eribete eriso):*
That which was lend out wholesome, has come back with one eye. (Borrowed items may not be properly cared for. One may lend out a cow but when it is returned it may be found maimed and even with one eye damaged.)

AMARIETA Y'EBINTO AO AO:

NAMES GIVEN TO VARIOUS THINGS

1. **Amarieta y'abakungu ba mogiti mochie (Amarieta y'abakungu banywomire aamo):**

Titles given to the wives of a polygamous man.

* *Mobuchaibu*   –   Senior wife (1st wife)
* *Nyamesanchu*   – favourite wife (2nd wife)
* *Nyabweri rogoro* – the one at the upper Kraal (3rd wife)
* *Nyabweri Maate* – the one at the lower Kraal (4th wife)
* *Nyageita* – the one at the gate (5th wife)

NB: If a man married more than five wives, the sixth was welcomed and lived with the 1st wife, the seventh with the second wife, the eighth with the third wife, and so on.

2. **Amarieta ye' chisimbagera (Amarieta ay'echiombe ao ao)**: Names given to types of cows (in the Abagusii community, cows were named according to their colours):

* *Nyabarati* - White and brown
* *Nyabisembe* - Brown with some black marks on abdomen.
* *Nyabunga* - Grey
* *Nyamasio* - Black with a white mark on the forehead.
* *Nyamagwari* - White and black stripes
* *Nyamonyinga* - Red ball
* *Nyamotika* - Brownish
* *Nyandabu* - Whitish
* *Nyang'era* - Blackish
* *Nyasamo* - Grey/white stripes
* *Nyasanako* - Red and dotted black
* *Nyasero* - Black/grayish
* *Nyaitosi* - Colour of mushroom

3 . **Amarieta ye'ribwogore ria Gusii:**

Names given to various stages of traditional liquor. (Liquor was brewed specifically to be drank by men during celebrations or after heavy task. It usually took about five days to be ready)

- *Ekenoko* – Fermented dough
- *Chinkara* – roasted dough in small fragments.
- *Ememera* – *wimbi* yeast
- *Enchoberi* – One day brew
- *Ributia* – Two-day's brew
- *Omokenonoko* – clear top ready liquior
- *Riseke* – Thick bottom ready liquor
- *Egechenge* – cold liquor
- *Egechuri* – warmed liquor (diluted with hot water)
- *Ey'enyongo ne chinkore* – of pot and straws.
- *Emeseke* – Dregs
- *Ekemite* – squeezed from dregs with flavour.
- *Omooto* – tasteless liquor, squeezed from dregs.
- *Omosuka* - recycled dregs for discarding.
- *Chinkama* – over brewed (stale liquor)

4. **Chibonyi chiare goonchorerigwa Gusii:**

Coins which were in common use in Gusii land:

- *Eropia* - 2 shilling silver coin
- *Enusi* - 1 shilling silver coin
- *Nyaigesa/Esomoni* - 50 cent silver coin
- *Mokanyamogendi* - 25 cent silver coin
- *Etongoro* - 10 cent copper coin
- *Ebaringi* - 5 cent copper coin
- *Eera* - 1 cent copper coin

5. ***Chinyongo Chiire Gusii:*** Gusii pottery.

•	*Embiiru*	– Largest water storage pot that may contain about 120 litres.
•	*Ensiongo*	– a pot used by women for fetching water (contains about 20 litres)
•	*Ekegancha*	– a pot used as storage for flour
•	*Ekeguru*	– a pot used by girls for fetching water (10 litres)
•	*Enyakaruga*	– a pot used for cooking Ugali
•	*Egetega*	– A pot used for cooking vegetables.
•	*Egetono*	– a small pot for serving especially milk
•	*Egetabo*	– a bowl-like pot used for serving vegetables or stew.

6. ***Emieri/Emechinini y'omwaka:***

(Emetienyi y'omwaka): Months of the year:

1.	*Egetamo*	- January
2.	*Omonuguno O'barema*	- February
3.	*Engatiato*	- March
4.	*Amaumuntia*	- April
5.	*Esagati*	- May
6.	*Ebwagi*	- June
7.	*Enkoromomi*	- July
8.	*Riete*	- August
9.	*Rigwata*	- September
10.	*Tureti a'kebaki*	- October
11.	*Egesunte gia 'Chache*	- November
12.	*Egesunte Kia Masaba*	- December

7. **Etiira ase ekegusii:** Compass directions.

•	*Sugusu*	-	North
•	*Irianyi*	-	South
•	*Mocha*	-	East
•	*Bosongo*	-	West

www.ingramcontent.com/pod-product-compliance
Lightning Source LLC
Chambersburg PA
CBHW020708270326
41928CB00005B/329